Makin' A
Joyful
Noise!

Tina Wash

WESTBOW
PRESS®
A DIVISION OF THOMAS NELSON
& ZONDERVAN

WestBow Press books may be ordered through booksellers or by contacting:

WestBow Press
A Division of Thomas Nelson & Zondervan
1663 Liberty Drive
Bloomington, IN 47403
www.westbowpress.com
844-714-3454

ISBN: 978-1-6642-3714-8 (sc)
ISBN: 978-1-6642-3713-1 (e)

Print information available on the last page.

WestBow Press rev. date: 06/21/2021

Welcome to Joy

Would you like to share in a day of Joy? Of peace? Of strength, of Comfort, of Plans for Goodness? *Makin' a Joyful Noise"* is a simple yet realistic approach to life. It is a recognition of the good that exists in everyday life as well as an encouragement to not only look for, but to express gratitude for the blessings one can easily overlook. Joy is always available. And that same joy can become the building blocks of the strength to face each new day. With each new day comes the provision of peace, comfort and the sense of purpose that is ours for the asking. We simply have to seek the Source of the blessings.

This text is intended to make you aware of, or to even be reminded that the life many of us desire is always present if we choose to see it. It is an inner contentment that allows one to breathe, to hope, to know that God is, and always will be in control. It is strength, and it is comfort. It is God's love and purpose for our lives, and it is ours for the *asking* - perhaps a better word is *accepting*. Know that God does use life's experiences to teach and strengthen us while preparing us for lives that truly have the opportunity to make this world a better place - for ourselves and for others. Daily we hear others offering guidance to make a better life – some methods are beneficial. Others are not. However, God's gift of joy can achieve that goal in ways too wonderful to imagine.

And yet, Joy is always a choice: acceptance or refusal.

I am sure you have heard it said that our circumstances "could always be worse." Too many end the thought there. It is important to consider that while circumstances could be worse, they have the potential to actually be better. We simply overlook the realities, the possibilities and the One who creates those possibilities. And, in addition, we fail to express the gratitude that both honors and warms the heart of the One who provides for us.

Today is certainly a good day to celebrate our blessings while saying "Thank You" to God who creates the Plan for our good and not for our harm! (Take a moment to read Jeremiah 29:11 in any translation and see the truth there.)

There is one additional piece of information I want to add right now. As a teacher I am fully aware that reading is a struggle for many. Whether a teenager or an adult, it is common for many to hesitate picking up a book to read. But I want you to enjoy the words provided within.

**That worthy goal includes my attempt
to encourage you, the reader,
to find an extra measure of comfort in this text,
as well as others, that contain the
messages God has prepared for you.**

It is formatted to prevent frustration in reading. Shorter length overall, shorter paragraphs allowing more white space on the page to prevent being overwhelmed by an overabundance of words. The white space allows your brain to focus on ideas present rather than miss the ideas that get lost in a simple case of 'too much at one time.' The chapters are shorter with key ideas repeated in bold print and set apart. The goal is to visibly note the main ideas to be remembered, or to help guide the reader in understanding what he or she just read. And, as one precious family member recently stated, "I figure I can at least read three pages, and when I find the next chapter is also short, I realize I can usually read 'just one more.'"

If you encounter a struggle in literally seeing the ideas or recognizing their unwritten explanations two strategies might help you while reading: do not consider speed or getting to the final punctuation your goal. Enjoy the journey. The second goal that cannot be denied is to have a dictionary nearby. Vocabulary contained within this text will rarely be difficult, but even in my Bible study I frequently use a dictionary to see the deeper meanings included in many of the words. While I may be familiar with a word, or understand its basic meaning in context, it is easy to overlook the deeper, emotional or motivational ideas in definitions 2, 3, or 4. The verses of the Bible can seem difficult to comprehend or more difficult yet, to create an interest in seeking the knowledge embodied within written words. Consider it a treasure hunt! You will find the riches if you only look. Oh, and certainly pray and marvel as you begin your own celebration!

I almost wish you could hear my voice, not because I am necessarily poised (as my Mother would have preferred) but because then you could hear my excitement!

It is then I can laugh at my silly stories and find that I am humbled as I realize how frequently I have gained new understanding and been impacted throughout the lifestyle application of the ideas presented.

Please join me for a celebration that
may just last for a lifetime!
And, let yourself treasure the Joy
provided each day of your life,
And always be faithful to say "Thank
You" for the Blessings

*"May the God of hope fill you with all joy
and peace as you trust in him,
so that you may overflow with hope by
the power of the Holy Spirit."*
Romans 15:13 NIV

Contents

I.

Chapter 1   Today is the day for Joy 1

Chapter 2   God Creates the Best Adventures!
                      Joy is only the beginning! 5

Chapter 3   His Steadfast Love Endures Forever 11

Chapter 4   Juggling Breakfast
                      A story of peanut butter… 17

Chapter 5   Tyranny – Time Pressure – Stress
                      Where is the Gratitude? 25

II.

Chapter 6   Playin' in the Band
                      God has already heard your
                      music, and He loves every note! 35

Chapter 7   Praise God with your voice –
            In singing, in teaching, and in
            shouting for joy!....................................43

Chapter 8   A Little Story... Sittin' in the
            Café on a Sunday afternoon or two
            As told by "A Fly on the Wall".............45

Chapter 9   Recognizin' Attitude can Make or Break Us
            My Choice and God's Grace................51

III.

Chapter 10 Good Morning, Lord!
            It's a new day; it's a new dawn.
            It is a new beginning............................61

Chapter 11 Makin' a joyful noise 63

Chapter 12 Serving Sounds like Work…
            Gladness Implies Purpose You
            Can Sing About 71

Chapter 13 Singin' Solo...77

Chapter 14 "Into each life a little rain must fall."

Chapter 15 Headin' Home
            To that place that may not be
            "Home Sweet Home"...........................87

IV.

Chapter 16   Playin' the Games Of Life
Of Desires and Guarantees... 95

Chapter 17   Singin' in the Valley 99

Chapter 18   And the Words of God still carry
Hope. And the Praises Must Still Ring
While Your Testimony
Encourages Others 105

Chapter 19   Speechless or Grateful? 107

Chapter 20   Playin' the Games Of Life
"What if...? 115

Chapter 21   Makin' the Climb 117

Chapter 22   Shoutin' from the Mountain Tops! 121

I.

**God Creates
the
Best Adventures!**

The Day for Joy
The Invitation is Given
Steadfast Love
Peanut Butter
Stress or Gratitude

1

---◆◆◆---

Today is the day for Joy

Today I shall sing.
Today I shall dance.
Today I shall praise my God and King.
Today I shall say Thank you, Lord!

Today is a day to celebrate! It is a day for Joyful Noise! Have you ever stopped to consider all the ways joyful noise is, or can be, expressed? In song, in excitement as one confesses love, celebrates a birthday or cheers on a favorite sports team. It may include the words, "I am so proud of you!" Think about that one-word text, 'Wow!' Then there is Whoo-Hoo! Yea! Outstanding! I am so excited about…! Hands clapping, drums beating, foot tapping. Hearts pounding. Children laughing. Can you think of others? Say them aloud right now…read this list aloud, quickly, allowing yourself to feel just a twinge of excitement before you continue.

Choose to say, maybe commit to, "Today I shall sing. Today I shall dance. Today I shall praise my God and King. Today I shall say "Thank You, Lord!" Don't be embarrassed or respond with "Maybe later." Even if you just settled in to read quietly for a while, take a breath and let yourself feel an overwhelming joy! You create it with your participation in reading the text aloud. You create it by recalling the good in your life, and for just this moment, forgetting the bad. You can deal with that a little later. Right now, just feel the joy, the encouragement, the excitement that God and the Bible offer to you throughout your lifetime.

In my first book, *A Bid for Eternity,* one is invited to God's Auction House to view and select all the magnificent gifts that God has provided for each of us. Needed items were given in advance, even before you or I were born, by a loving God who knew and planned for our lives - long before we arrived on this earth. God is always prepared – therefore we can be prepared if we are willing to depend upon Him and trust Him with our daily lives - as well as our future.

Even if the past few sentences are all you know of God's plans for your life, surely the need for joy and gratitude is due today and always. And, just as we are taught to say "Thank you" for a gift received, so too, we must let God hear our Thank You and our Praises for a love that cannot be discounted.

Would you join me for a celebration of God, with a joyful noise in our praises and in our gratitude? Will you sing of His great plans for your life? Will your heart be allowed the fullness of a joy that simply must be expressed? Will you offer all you are and all you have to honor Him? Will you survey all your life's accomplishments and treasures, and say Thank You?

**As you rush through your morning,
your responsibilities, your decisions and your dreams
will you take the time to acknowledge the
One who guides you with a loving hand?**

*You will notice throughout this book
the tone is conversational;
the format is designed to encourage interaction
with the understanding presented.
Shorter chapters to encourage reading despite busy schedules,
Reviews and intentional repetition to encourage
application of ideas presented.*

*We all have more to learn and certainly
more joy to experience.
God has more to teach, and life will
always present opportunities
to apply God's loving and insightful lessons.*

*It is my hope that your life will certainly be filled with the joy
that our world is striving so hard to find.
It is entirely possible that you will even have joy left over
to share with others as well!
In fact, may I state, it is a promise!*

2

God Creates the Best Adventures!

**The Invitation has been given.
Joy is only the beginning!**

Have you ever dreamed of accomplishing something great? for God? For anyone? For the world? Can you recognize 'possibilities,' only to immediately see 'reality' attempting to discourage you? Do you ever question why others' definition of reality seems to overshadow God's reality?

In spite of this, have you dared to try?

Unfortunately, defeat rather than success occurs more often than not, but those who are willing to risk everything for a relationship with God, who are willing to accept that one's life may seem unusual to others, and who choose to be bold in sharing their belief in God will find excitement, adventure, and incredible joy in the journey. The *Merriam*

Tina Wash

Webster Dictionary online defines adventure as *"an exciting or noteworthy event that one experiences firsthand."*

Isn't living excitement, adventure, and incredible joy better than just imagining it?

It seems fair to say that we learn more about life as we live it. We recognize what it means to be Actively Engaged in life as we know it. We realize there is more to be Appreciated. We begin to see there was a difference when we were Prepared to live a life worthy of respect versus when we are found unprepared. We Understand more, and we become more Understanding of others. We sometimes regret not having appreciated our opportunities more; we regret that sometimes "slow" realization or our rejection of the fact that God truly is the source of all blessings. However, as we mature and grow in our knowledge of God it becomes easier to see that God working in our daily lives deserves an even more obvious, more complete love on our part, and that love deserves to be expressed with true joy and resounding gratitude.

I have realized the highlight of seeing God at work in daily life deserves an even more obvious, more complete and utter gratitude on my part. I actually have known this for a lifetime, but recently I have been convicted to acknowledge God's goodness much, much, much more. Why is it that we don't always recognize our blessings until after the fact?

With each new acknowledgement of His work in my life I am reminded again of Psalm 100 and my introduction to it in a 4th grade Sunday School department. All members were encouraged, instructed, rehearsed, and given promises of a red King James Presentation Bible as a reward if they could recite that Psalm 100 with perfection - in hopes that we would remember the words throughout our lifetime. It worked. I still have that Bible and am reminded of those words on a regular basis. As I recite that chapter aloud, I realize that is what I want others to hear, to learn, and to be reminded of.

The translation below is not the King James Version I memorized as a child (that will follow in a later chapter), but when I saw this translation I was simply filled with an overwhelming joy and excitement! And I want to share it with you. The meaning is the same, and the level of joy seems perfect to begin a book filled with gratitude and praise. What an exciting way to begin a new adventure with God!

Psalm 100:1-5
from The Message

"On your feet now—applaud God!
Bring a gift of laughter,
Sing yourselves into his presence.
Know this: God is God, and God, God.
He made us; we didn't make him.
We're his people, his well-tended sheep.
Enter with the password: "Thank you!"
Make yourselves at home, talking praise.
Thank him. Worship him.
For God is sheer beauty,
all-generous in love,
loyal always and ever."

Please take the time to simply breathe in the words. Smile as you read them aloud. Feel your heart beating a little faster. The words are encouraging. They are factual. They are fun. They deserve a fuller understanding, and they certainly deserve a fuller application in all of our lives. The words are strong, and *they allow you to be strong*.

Take time to enjoy God's goodness, as well as allow yourself to be motivated and willing to do as the scriptures say. Close your eyes and see the images contained in Psalm 100. Learn about the fuller, contextual meaning of being God's people, His "well-tended sheep." Feel the wonder of the words as you read and commit them to memory. Know and repeat the words to others, whether in celebration, encouragement, or in teaching. Enjoy the person of God as you learn more about His love for you…

Always be aware that gratitude is one of the best ways to show love and caring for the blessings we receive. And it should be given joyously – not begrudgingly or in resentment or without total sincerity. It is a time of both joy and appreciation and respect for the One who has given so freely, so wisely. Who deserves our gratitude more than God?

Take a minute to re-read Psalm 100 from *The Message* printed in this chapter. Pay special note to the password given. And what was it? Saying "Thank You!" for all that is and has been your life. And for all that your life will be in the future.

You are invited to join me
For an exciting, possibly unusual experience…
At times it may require risk, a little boldness,

and certainly much, much gratitude
for God's wisdom and care.

Enter with the Password and make yourself at home...
One more round of applause for
God as we continue, please.

3

---- ⟨⟩ ----

His Steadfast Love
Endures Forever

"For the Lord is good; His mercy is everlasting:
and His truth endureth to all generations."
Psalm 100:5 KJV

As with any text it may be tempting to read quickly and move on to completing the passage or text, but please take a moment to consider the words printed above. Could those words be included in your joyful noise to God on a regular basis? Are they worthy of repeating to friends and family, to the world? How is your understanding of that as a joyful noise? Is it possible gladness has been overcome by responsibility? Are additional voice lessons required? Consider the images created by the word "endureth?" Think about that, and let's "talk."

In Bible study I find it beneficial to begin a mental and prayerful dialogue as I try to understand what is written and follow that with its application to life as I know it.

Let me encourage you now to do the same, and let's begin with the word "noise." If you look it up in the dictionary its definition may be a negative which does not correlate with the verse above. Please don't stop there…Noise alone can create stress, drown out something one needs to learn from, create a barrier to what one is hoping to learn.

However, the true meaning will never be obvious unless one looks carefully at the descriptors occurring with the "noise." In this case, the adjective is "joyful." And that makes all the difference in understanding! Joy. Joy comes from the Lord. Joy is shared by those who receive it willingly. Joy seems to be mankind's goal, and yet, the true joy only comes in knowing the source of all understanding, God. That knowledge alone gives one the encouragement to praise, to sing, to celebrate and appreciate the only One who can fully explain the complete meaning of joy!

Making a joyful noise can take many forms. The outward expression of one's grateful attitude – even in midst of hardship. The smile that elicits the smiles of others, especially when your smile is the only one some see all day. The love that surges as you see one in need and reach out to help. The hope that is realized when one is reminded that God is still in control, that Jesus still loves, that the Bible still carries only truth. Those simple acts resonate throughout the universe and warm the heart of God.

And, don't forget the sound of boots marching in step with the Lord. Determined, dedicated, and committed to follow their "Commander." Marching onward in discipline despite any and all circumstances. Then there are those brave ones who speak the truth of God and lead others to a relationship with Jesus despite fear. There are the voices ringing from the choir who reach hearts with their words while they share the wonder and joy of all God has done within their music.

I need to insert "However" at this point. It is important all of us remember that making a joyful noise to God does not require scholarly research or musical training or require that our joyful noise fit the parameters or guidelines of others – it is your personal desire to reach out to Him that brings the joy. It is the songs sung off-key in the shower if a heart is reaching out to or celebrating God. It is the wrong notes of our lives sung in the midst of uncertainty or mistakes while still reaching out in prayer and confession. The notes are not required to be beautiful to all; they are simply sung to the One who loves and forgives and hears the voices of ones He loves so very much.

Psalm 100:1 KJV says, "Make a joyful noise unto the Lord all ye lands." Note the last three words of that verse. This sounds like a general call to all nations, all peoples, all of nature to worship God. That is what God truly desires. David is encouraging each and every one who hears to make a joyful noise to the one and only God. Show God your gratitude! Speak His name in prayer and in testimony. It may just be singing praise while reaching out to others to join in.

However, I also think the verse has an additional, very personal meaning. In this world we are given, and responsible for, a great deal on a daily basis. God is designating what I am personally responsible for, not just a part of my life but every facet of it. I believe that all I have and all I desire is considered my land. And it is up to me to be a good steward of it. I must recognize that my possessions, my real estate, my treasures and my pride are placed in my life so that I might have the opportunity to celebrate God. They must never replace God.

If we make decisions contrary to God's laws, then noise does begin to take on that unpleasant tone of just negative noise. It is up to you and me to monitor all noises that emanate from our lives – for God's benefit and for ours. We are responsible for the adjectives we attach.

Can I share a personal memory? My favorite hymn has been *"All Creatures of our God and King"* in the Baptist Hymnal by Convention Press since childhood. I remember standing in church, with the sun shining through those very tall stained-glass windows - sunbeams dancing on the faces of those nearby, noting the presence of the deacons sitting on the first row – a position of authority and humility, and stopping occasionally as I listened to the other voices singing with joy. (I could not listen for long though, because I truly enjoyed singing the words myself – typical six-year-old) And then, there were the moments my eyes began to explore the Rose Window above the balcony, the elevated ceiling and shining, almost dignified lights as we reached the lines: "lift up your voice and with us sing, Oh, Oh Praise Him! Alleluia." Those were my favorite Sundays. I am convinced Mother had noted the inclusion of that hymn in the bulletin and then moved all of us to the 6th row where the sunbeams danced the liveliest. She never acknowledged the purpose for the moves when she made them, but she watched my joy and did all she could to insure I knew the One who created that joy. That was what she considered her "land."

Your joyful noise may be the decision to not live a divided life with priorities taking a variety of forms, while leaving God at the bottom of the list. It may be tears shed in sorrow or in an effort to wash away failures. It may be a broken heart reaching out for comfort. It may even be a simple "I love You, Lord" spoken quietly in prayer. If you are seeking God in honesty and stating your decision to choose Him above all others – you are making that joyful noise that God wants to hear from all of us.

It is important to note that there are many who epitomize the life available if we do dedicate all our own "lands", the lives we want to live, the people we want to be – if only we could. And we can, if we choose.

The hymn, *"Just As I Am"* in the Baptist Hymnal by Convention Press seems to cover a great deal of the struggles humans face. But it is more. It is a request to be accepted and an effort to become what God anticipated our lives to be. It is an acknowledgement that "all I need in thee to find..." and the announcement that we are on our way! It is another of my favorites, sung for so many years, by memory, and only now considering every specific element that works as a whole to take us into conversation with God. Acceptance despite our sin, Confidence that God still loves, He will forgive, and He is the source of all we truly need. It is a Declaration of our understanding of who God is. And it is Commitment on our part as well as a willingness to enter His presence. Let your Praise and Gratitude glorify God.

That is why we sing – regardless of the quality of our voices, regardless of needing to hum a few phrases because we forgot the words, regardless of where we are or who we are with. We choose to praise God because He deserves to hear it – regardless of our singing ability. He hears the sound our heartstrings. And He loves it!

**"Enter into His gates with thanksgiving and
into His courts with praise." Ps 100:4 KJV**

God is always present in our lives, in every moment, every joy, every struggle and offering, yet another opportunity to openly state that He will meet our needs. That deserves gratitude, acceptance of God's instruction, and prayer to ensure each gift is used wisely and in accordance with the perfect plans God has for your life.

But you must still choose to open wide any gate that prevents you from entering into God's presence. Acknowledge that sins may look tempting but seek to destroy. Pray for God's strength that allows you to stand strong. Make the hard choices. Say "No." Turn and walk away…even if you have to crawl. It is a choice like any other. Sometimes difficult, sometimes not. Trust the words of your Bible.

Know that you are always under the watchful, protective eye of God.

4

Juggling Breakfast

A story of peanut butter...

"Praise the Lord. Sing to the Lord a new song,
His praise in the assembly of His faithful people."
Psalm 149:1 ESV

We are told to start our days with a healthy breakfast – today I tried. I really want to share the experience if I may, because healthy does not always guarantee the ideal mealtime.

My breakfast consisted of an apple, peanut butter, and hot coffee. And of course, my dog Ranger standing close by. Typically, breakfast is eaten in front of my Bible with pen in hand and a journal nearby. Will you join me at the breakfast table?

> I open my Bible to Psalm 149. Coffee, apple
> and peanut butter nearby.

Need to eat apple and/or peanut butter first so coffee does not hurt my stomach.

Need hot coffee to wake me up so can concentrate on the Bible in front of me.

Decide to drink coffee quickly, because I simply do not enjoy cold coffee.

Ranger, my little dog, smells the peanut butter and shows up at my feet in hopes of a bite.

And then, inspiration strikes; I need to write it down before I forget.

Yet, I begin to wonder, 'is my coffee getting cold?'

Take another sip of coffee, and notice the apple is beginning to turn brown from neglect.

Ranger sees me take a bite and insists on his.

I once again need coffee to lessen the sweetness of the apple and peanut butter.

Ranger notifies me that he wants another bite also.

So, I take one as well, but the apple has turned brown. I take a last bite of peanut butter.

Coffee has grown cold - Journal virtually empty. Seems breakfast is over.

And it has not been relaxing at all!

The Bible still says, *"Sing to the Lord a new song."* Psalm 149:1 ESV.
How can I sing with peanut butter in my mouth?

Please note: the above anecdote is best read out loud and quickly if you hope to truly understand the "mood." Now, if your breakfast is made up of yogurt or eggs, those items can typically be swallowed more smoothly, and the singing can be happening sooner. I, on the other hand, was attempting to sing through the peanut butter but found it easier to continue writing with a cold coffee cup in hand and a Bible before me, all the while growing more and more frustrated. Ranger had even grown impatient and finally returned to his bed.

And, the Bible still stands before me.

I notice peanut butter on my finger. Where is my napkin? Must be on the floor. You know peanut butter has always been messy, and now I cannot even find my napkin on the floor! Hmmm, believe there is a mystery to be solved…. Have to resist the temptation to grab a magnifying glass to see if the napkin shrunk on the way down. My next impulse is to accuse Ranger of stealing the napkin away to his bed, to shred it, swallow parts of it and choke when he realizes a napkin is not intended as dessert. And the coffee cup is now cold and empty.

But the Bible still stands before me.

I begin to wonder if God is laughing at my efforts to keep everything clean, sequential, and organized. I suppose I never considered the comical aspect of trying to satisfy my desire for apples and peanut butter, my insistence on HOT coffee, my responsibility to share with Ranger, all the while keeping my fingers clean – only to lose my napkin.

Seriously, when did breakfast become a teaching moment? Today… God is always teaching; it is simply up to us to pay attention and learn. I made plans; Ranger wanted to be a part. Coffee required urgency, and messes needed a napkin. I lost the napkin, or "someone" attempted to hide that napkin from me.

But, my Bible still stood on the table before me.

And suddenly, I saw the parallel. I had sat down with a plan perfectly laid out. There was too much to handle at one time, at least too much to handle within the parameters I had set for the perfect, relaxing breakfast. Suddenly, another in "need" showed up. The one thing I thought I could rely on was hot coffee to insure I could understand the Bible verse. My distracting desire for more was interrupted by another's need. I created a bit of a mess, only to find my "get out of peanut butter card" had disappeared! With a little imagination can you see the application to self-made plans for life?

And, the Bible still stands on the table before me.

One, relaxation will never be possible if one gives in to the "Tyranny of the Urgent." That phrase is the title from the book written by Charles E. Hummel. Two, is personal relaxation and comfort supposed to be the objective when others are in need? I made plans. Ranger wanted to be a part, and he was genuinely hungry. Coffee required urgency; messes needed a napkin – that very napkin *I* had 'lost' due to carelessness. Immediate response was to accuse another of attempting to hide that napkin from me.

But my Bible still stood before me.

"For I know the plans I have for you, declares the Lord" Jeremiah 29:11 NIV. Perhaps the priority was, and the peace would have been in the Bible standing before me. But I was focused on other things, on my own plans.

Psalms 37:4 KJV says, "and He shall give you the desires of your heart." Right then I only wanted my peanut butter and to enjoy it without interference. The thing about that verse is that one must read the beginning of the verse as well: "Delight thyself also in the Lord; and..." Have you ever noticed that the things mankind desires are temporary, wonderful in the moment but begin to fade (grow cold) or create problems soon after?

One very important concept that all Christians must understand is that our enthusiasm will draw others to us. In the overall scheme of things, I cannot fault Ranger for the insistent desire for his own bite of peanut butter. Afterall, I am the one who introduced him to it.

What if the same enthusiasm for a relaxing breakfast encompassed sharing our faith? Even if our witness brings others to Christ would we, or do we ever try to ignore others who are hungry for knowledge of God, struggling or lost without any hope and direction if or when they appear at an inconvenient time? Young Christians should never have to schedule appointments; those without a relationship with God should never have to question if Christians truly follow God's example of love.

Read again the "Feeding of the Five Thousand" in Matthew 14:13-21. Look at the example, the attitude and the miracle of Jesus who *met them at the point of their need*. I only had to share with one, my little dog, and I couldn't manage that when I was hungry and even more worried about hot coffee! Surely the disciples' mouths watered as they distributed the fish and bread, yet there is no note of them tending to their own hunger before all were fed.

Exodus 20: 3 KJV says, "Thou shalt have no other gods before me." Can you even imagine a quiet whisper in Moses' ear on the day God's Commandments were written in stone warning that peanut butter might one day attempt to control someone's Bible Study? No! While hearing from God, the one true God, do you think Moses would have chosen to interrupt by sharing his desire for hot coffee to start the day? Absolutely NOT. That is actually absurd… and yet, consider the responsibilities of your workplace, your home, your witness and mankind's desire to determine what is needed before one can worship God. Do we offer to please God if He will allow us to be pleased?

Do we make bargains with God? Do our desires take precedence over salvation, or witness, or compassion, or of studying that Bible that still stands before us?

And now, the lesson is written as a reminder, a caution and just one silly example of our plans for our lives creating more anxiety, failure, more stress than God ever planned. Oh, I still needed that napkin for the peanut butter still on my fingers - and now on the pages of my journal. That napkin can be *our* attempts to "clean" up our lives – for whatever reason that makes us aware life can be messy. Spoiler alert: attempts to "perfect" one's own life rarely work.

However, Jesus' ability to clear away the messes and leave our hands "clean" to serve Him will always work if we only realize that maybe the true lesson of "apples and peanut butter, hot coffee, and messy, disappearing napkins" is that Jesus has already addressed the messes we create. He teaches in our Bible, and we must listen. He will choose anything that can gain our attention and, softly and gently, allow us to recognize the parallels.

After all, that Bible is still standing before us.

As I closed out that morning of stress, silliness, and understanding I stood with journal in hand, gathered my materials, and I heard myself screaming, "Where did that napkin come from?!!?" I was certainly choosing to look for it when I needed it. Can we parallel that with rushing to God to help with the urgency that often controls our days, yet not attempting to learn more of our Bible when life is not occurring just as we would hope. I had really tried but could not find that napkin on my own! It turns out that Ranger ("another") was not guilty after all – that qualified as false judgment on my part. Hmmm, false judgment, impatience created by desiring breakfast progress as I had planned, my refusal to enjoy cold coffee, my attempts to ignore a hungry puppy, and failing to touch and read my Bible....and where had my napkin been? Underneath my Bible.

**That Bible that stood before me throughout...
Guarding that which I still needed
but could not find on my own.**

5

─────◦◦◦◦─────

Tyranny – Time
Pressure – Stress

Where is the Gratitude?

"Shout for joy to God, all the earth;
sing the glory of His name;
give to Him glorious praise!"
Psalm 66:1-2 ESV

God Deserves So Much More Than We Often Choose to Give. He deserves our gratitude, our joy, our recognition of him. Regardless of perfect plans, or lack of awareness. Every single one of us has much to be grateful for. That is truth. It is true despite difficulties you may be living through right now. It is true whether we want to admit it or not. However, have you ever noticed how often life attempts to distract us - even as we choose to thank God for His blessings?

**Schedules, problems, responsibilities, and
the resulting stress seeks to divert**

**our attention away from the joy, peace,
the promises and gifts of God.
For that reason, we must recognize our
obligation to offer gratitude to God
for the wisdom of our Bible, for the
Blessings given, FIRST –
Whether we have recognized them
or not. They are there.
Whether we have decided to appreciate
them or not. They are still given.
Whether we understand them or not,
His blessings are always present.**

Call it good manners. Call it spiritual maturity. Call it obligation. You may choose the wording, but please understand it is important. God deserves at least that. He deserves so much more as well. *Stop* this moment and *consider* some of the undeserved favor you have experienced. *Think* about the possible consequences of your sin and give thanks for the undeserved mercy. *Remember* the "folly" of your youth and look where you are today. Regret your mistakes and *celebrate* the safety and love God provided despite your efforts to create the opposite of safety and love. Stop, consider, think, remember, celebrate. Take a moment to express your gratitude *to* God. And let yourself experience the joy God offers!

Throughout life we are all given opportunities to make a difference in this world, but that same life that many want to improve also contains elements demanding attention immediately - regardless of other priorities, regardless of time constraints, regardless of the need to worship, regardless of the obligation to say, "Thank You, Lord." The need to study one's Bible, or to even sit for a few moments in prayer can be easily overlooked. Therefore, choices have to be made.

In 1969, Charles E. Hummel wrote *The Tyranny of the Urgent.* The title alone may cause you to pause and identify with the reality of those words. That text is often an integral part of several college courses "planning for success" in the workplace. Say that title aloud: doesn't it just roll of the tongue? I admit that I love just saying it; the truth cannot be denied. I would even suggest that if you are breathing today, you have already experienced that same challenge in your life, just since you woke up. Hummel described it as the difference between what may appear urgent at any point in one's day and what is truly important in the moment.

Merriam Webster defines important as "marked by or indicative of significant worth or consequence; valuable in content or relationship." Consider what is important in the life you are leading today. Your list may be long, but is God included anywhere in that list? Could you really succeed at everything else on your list if He is not? Is there anything on your list that strengthens your relationship with Him? Life moves quickly. Simply juggling all responsibilities is difficult, sometimes overwhelming, and can often diminish one's joy. God is the one who puts that unequaled joy back into the daily responsibilities. By the way, He also adds the organizational skills, the wisdom, and the strength to overcome the stress.... Doesn't that deserve gratitude?

Once we realize the competition for the important elements of our lives,

the celebrations of God, for God, and with God can begin – even if the gratitude is for that short, five-minute window when your shoulders relax, your heartbeat slows to normal, and there is just a touch of joy tugging at the corners of your mouth.

This morning, I reviewed Hummel's text on my Kindle to insure it actually said what I remembered – no more use of a simple, lofty sounding quote but an in-depth approach that acknowledges needed priorities in our lives. The text really is worthy of a read. I also noticed an online "comment" summarizing the text as "all religious stuff" and offering to save future readers the two bucks…Wait! Shouldn't that BE the focus? Shouldn't we all be aware of how often God is given second, or even third place in our lives? Is that clever little phrase actually full of great wisdom, self-realization? Could it be your "Call to Arms" to reset priorities, focus first on God and trust that everything else can wait when compared to the majesty, the love, the power, the grace, and the glory of God?

One thing I want to point out, or confess, or identify with others, is that when solutions to problems, or relief from hurt or safety concerns occur, far too many of us give into the temptation to run to others to celebrate good news or success immediately. Before we share our gratitude with God. Before we take the time to just relax in God's presence, to say 'Thank You' for this special time in my hectic life." Before we stand and acknowledge that we understand He never left us; He never let us be fully destroyed; He never gave up the hope that those five-minute windows might just turn into extended prayer times…and a deeper, more loving relationship with Him. Allow God the opportunity to celebrate with you FIRST.

And then, only after expressing gratitude for the sheer joy provided in our lives, does it become important to shout "about" that same Joy to others.

Understand it is human nature to run to others, to tell them about that incredible, joyous few minutes that you experienced. Totally understandable, totally human. The conversations begin with, "I can't wait to share!" It is common and good to begin group prayer times with "Are there any praises?" And there always are – Thank you, Lord! Working with various age groups throughout the years and listening to the praises of others I began to see a great deal of my story-telling techniques in others. We all believed that sharing praises really did include giving all pertinent information as to why that subject was truly a 'praise.' Even if that pertinent information began with childhood and continued throughout a lifetime, with pauses for important details along the way. Please know, Lighthouse Class, *I am laughing **with** you not at you.*

Others begin the praise and then try to determine How or Why something good occurred. Too often the final determination is "I did it." "I" succeeded. "I" planned it… "I, I, I"

Rather than attempting to gain the credit, we ought to give and seek to give all gratitude to God. Replace those "I" statements with "God has blessed me yet again! Everything else flowed through that act of God. I truly have been blessed by God." We must want others to be aware of how gracious and exciting God is. That is joy "about" God.

All that comes our way is determined by Him...the treasure, the love, the discipline, the mercy, the instruction, the grace, the love, and most of all, the Salvation. All credit is due to Him, and all is given in a love that "surpasses all understanding." Ephesians 3:19 ESV.

God may ask you to be a "partner" in bringing His will to fruition – and that is an incredible honor. But, it will never be intended to remove God's ownership of the Plan.

Philippians 4:19-20 ESV states it plainly, "And my God will supply every need of yours according to His riches in glory in Christ Jesus. To our God and Father be glory forever and ever." You have been blessed and need to give Him the glory. I promise. Consider Malachi 3:10 ESV. set in a specific time in biblical history but, as always, applicable to life as we know it: "Bring the full tithe into the storehouse that there may be food in my house. And thereby put me to the test, says the Lord of hosts, if I will not open the windows of heaven for you and pour down for you a blessing until there is no more need." While not applying a literal definition of the use of the word "Tithe," could that principle also be utilized in your praise and love for Him being shared with others? If only 10% of our conversation with others included gratitude and praise for God... If only 10% of our conversations spoke of Jesus's love... Can you imagine the impact on a world struggling to simply exist? 10%.

Yet, we still struggle to sit still long enough to give God

the credit for "every good and perfect gift." James 1:17 KJV. One, there are others to tell others our exciting news! Two, sitting still in reverence may be hard when excited. Three, we simply or deliberately choose to forget who truly deserves the credit. Not one of those is justification for a lack of gratitude - in front of others - to the One who makes all things possible.

One additional note: Just as mankind is quick to accept the praise for ourselves, we are often even quicker to lay the blame for our failures, mistakes, belligerence and anger as well as the results of our own sin at the feet of God. Some characterize God as the source of the ensuing difficulty – they claim to have been cursed, hurt, zapped, abandoned, denied, punished, treated unfairly, or ignored by God. By the way, these conversations tend to last longer, be repeated more often, and manipulated to elicit sympathy for self or justification for anger. Sometimes 50% or more? That attempt to lay the blame elsewhere is given reign far more often than the acknowledgement that gratitude should be given to God first and foremost. It should be, therefore we all must choose to do so. At least 10%. May I suggest a simple prayer to acknowledge how important God is in your life? And identify the key elements...

"Lord, I know you still love me; Your intent will never be to destroy me.
(Fact that cannot be denied. Faith to believe it. and Gratitude for the Blessings.)

I know that. And I choose to fully trust it.

(Note that with verbal practice your
conviction of that statement will grow.)

**I may not fully appreciate or understand
the lessons right now,**
(That is honesty needed in relationship.)

**but I know they are Your efforts to provide
me the strength to follow You,
and to provide the opportunity for others
to see You through my actions."**

II.

The Band is growing;
the opportunities for
worship
are endless, & yours is
a voice God is waiting for.

Playin' in the Band
Praisin' God with your voice
Sittin' in a Café
Recognizin' Attitude

6

Playin' in the Band

**God has already heard your music,
and He loves every note!**

*"When I look at Your heavens, the work of your fingers,
The moon and the stars, which you have set in place,
What is man that You are mindful of Him?"*
Psalm 16:3-4a ESV

Many, many psalms have been incorporated into praise and worship songs, majestic choral presentations and included in the verses of familiar hymns. There is a beauty in those words. If you have never taken the time to devote your reading to the book of Psalms let me begin to encourage you to do so. You may be surprised at just how many of those verses are already familiar because you have sung them before; you have heard the words enough to quote them yourself even if you do not remember their source. We know David from his days as a shepherd through his days as one who struggles and throughout his reign as King.

One element that seems almost natural to his life was the music that lifted his soul, comforted him, and praised the God he loved.

One instrument mentioned in the Bible and associated most often with David is the lyre or harp, a 10-stringed, portable instrument. If you take the time to research that instrument you will see why – it was easier to carry with the shepherds as they protected their flocks throughout the night. The music provided proved soothing comfort not only to David but to the sheep as well. And it provided *audible praise for God*.

Surrounded by the stillness that allows one to see and hear God without distraction, to gaze upon the moon and stars lighting the earth, and to recognize the majesty of God visually, spiritually and without competition, except for maybe a lamb gone astray, David often found the opportunity to pray and praise God. There was time. There was encouragement from Nature to worship God. There was the Peace that allows one to see and feel God's spirit without the barriers that stress so often creates.

For David, looking into the heavens insured that he could never deny God's glory in the skies above. He needed only to look at his flocks to see his reason for being in that moment – his purpose was to protect. He needed only to acknowledge and express his love for God, because David understood who God is, all God had already done in his life, and David was fully aware that God had plans and a purpose for his life, regardless.

Do you have that same confidence in God? Is there enough time during busy days to exhibit it? Or do we live in a world that sometimes seems out of control? Do you ever just wish for a simple, uninterrupted time to talk with God but cannot find it or Him? It is when we give into stress, the frantic 'doing,' and distractions of mankind's world that God seems far away. Focus instead on the peace and tranquility and provision that God provides.

Does anyone today carry a 10-string harp in the back pocket to soothe the soul or to praise God in the midst of the day? If so, please let me know! However, God still has taken steps to ensure we may always enter His presence without distraction. Yes, it involves a choice, and yes, it is always a wise choice as well. In *Sacred Pathways*, Gary Thomas explains nine "spiritual temperaments" that God has already placed within us to allow communication with God at any time, regardless. Thomas explains spiritual temperaments in an attempt "to help us understand how we can best relate to God so we can develop new ways of drawing near to Him." Much like our spiritual gifts explained in I Corinthians 12, God has already guaranteed that we have all we need inside us to not only to serve Him but to reach out to Him as well. Understanding who we are and the importance of relationship with God, it is comforting to know we need never lose contact with God whenever we need Him, His Wisdom, His Love, His Protection and to simply say we Love Him. We just need to know where to look, and how to turn our eyes away from the chaos.

Note that the gift is already a part of who we are, but it is also up to us to develop it, to practice it, and to acknowledge a trust that we will never be unable to communicate with God. There is a great deal being said in that last sentence. "Acknowledge" means admitting you know God will "never leave you or forsake you," Deuteronomy 31:8 KJV. Note the word "trust." It is a choice; it is strengthened by its use; it is edifying, and it is exciting. The "never be unable to communicate" is a guarantee, a commitment made by the God of the Universe in advance. "God" – Creator, Teacher, Protector, Judge and Loving Father…all that we ever truly hope for in a Friend.

Now back to Gary Thomas' book. It amazed me to see my life in print, describing how much I enjoy being in nature, away from all the concrete. As I read the chapter on "Naturalists" my eyes began to tear up just as they do when I leave the stress, the hurt, the confusion or the exhaustion to walk outside and feel that relaxing peace that is soon followed by the tears of gratitude as I realize God is right beside me and simply enjoying our conversations. That is who I am. That is *my* line of direct communication that has the blessing of seeing the trees, hearing the birds, feeling the warmth of the sun or seeing the beauty of the moon. God created them all for our benefit as well as His. And you and I get to enjoy them fully! Your temperament may be different than mine (there are nine according to Gary Thomas), and I would encourage you to be amazed as you learn more about God's gifts. If you are aware of your spiritual gifts as listed in 1st Corinthians 12 you just might find out how the person already existing within you is not only 'dressed' for God's work but has also received a direct line of communication any time it is needed or desired.

How can this encourage you to take your position "Playin' in the Band?" First of all, you must have a **true belief in God**. Believe He made you to be a part of a bigger plan. His Plan. Live in and through the belief God has in you. Secondly, God has already heard your "music", and He loves every note. Really. Instead of doubt or insecurity, say Thank You and **accept all He has given you in advance** to prepare you for this day, this moment in time. Never overlook Jesus' forgiveness of sin and invitation to eternal life – that is what has made you so very, very special. Pick your own style of "music," and sing loudly and graciously to all who pass by.

Understand that your life is treasured by God. And realize that you were created for a purpose greater than any human agenda could create. Know that you can trust Him to bang the drum to allow you to stay in step with Him. His every drumbeat keeps the music flowing through your heart. Share it.

> **You were created to worship God and bring His love into the world.**

And you may do so through music, writing, teaching or caring, to name only a few. Whatever, wherever God directs will be perfect. I guarantee it. Listen to His Voice and share His Love with the world through whatever your voice is led to "sing." Possibilities and beautiful "music" are simply waiting to be heard.

> **The Band is growing; the opportunities for worship are endless, and yours is a voice God is waiting for.**

There is third component, one that is vital to preventing the distractions that only seek to destroy the person God created you to be; it is to realize your **need for God.** He alone contains the necessary wisdom to navigate the pitfalls of this world. He alone has the power and understanding we need on a daily basis. He is the source of needed strength and mercy. He composed the beautiful music. Every song God gives us to sing is worthy of our attention, our gratitude and the acknowledgement that "every good and perfect gift is from above..." James 1:17 NIV.

You must also understand the need for caution as you daily encounter timely and insightful (and exciting) guidance...never allow pride to govern your words or actions. That beautiful voice - God provided it. Those words of wisdom - He taught you the lessons others need to hear. That ability to connect with others, to nurture others, to care for the sick and lonely - each heartbeat was given by God. Yes, you may be confident in your efforts, but remember that many if not all were developed as God gave you opportunity to learn. You may look back with joy or excitement on your accomplishments; that is a good and wonderful feeling. However, never even consider that God had ignored your process so that you could be worthy of all the praise and honor. That temptation has the power to destroy all the blessings of God in your life and the lives of others. Relying on God, allowing God to be God, accepting that you have gifts and abilities that can only be extraordinary if you are willing to acknowledge God in all you do and all you say does not make you weak. It makes you blessed, prepared, able to act with confidence, and needed in a world that is looking for answers and a little bit of beautiful music.

**You and God together have so very,
very much to offer this world.
Step forward and do as God directs.**

All has been given as encouragement for a successful life, a successful 'career' in the band, and days of purpose. Now, take a deep breath and begin to feel the excitement of your journey. It is time for you to **discover** what your future with God holds! Spend time with Him so no joy or opportunity is missed. Read your Bible and be amazed at who God is. Listen to Him more closely as He comforts and directs your path. Pray continually – formally if you desire or simple, incomplete sentences as your thoughts pour out, but also listen as God speaks to you in that moment. And then, spend your days on a wondrous treasure hunt! Look for God in the midst of business meetings. Look for God and His insight in conversations, in your surroundings, in your goals, in your words and in your heart. Look for Him in the grocery store or on the freeway! Look for God as you open your front door each morning. Take note of all He is doing and join His Band. Look for Him – **He is always nearby**.

*"It is the Lord who goes before you.
He will be with you; He will not leave you or forsake you.
Do not fear or be dismayed."*
Deuteronomy 31:8 ESV

7

〰〰

Praise God with your voice –

In singing, in teaching, and in shouting for joy!

*Let others hear your voice; let them be
drawn to your words and your faith.*

*Read scripture aloud.
Let scripture become a part of your witness,
Let it be evidence of your faith – and your reassurance.*

*Let others hear, with conviction, the words
that bring life and hope and wisdom.
Let others see it is your choice to show God
that His words matter to you –
and let those same words be within hearing range of others.
Your voice may be the only way some can "hear" God's Word.*

Pray aloud.
Acknowledge WHO you are praying to!
No need to fear others; simply let them
enjoy your conversations with God.
Allow them to learn from your relationship with God.
Seek wisdom from God while expressing your need –
then speak His answers, His comfort, His wisdom aloud
so that others may hear.
Express your gratitude aloud – in fact, do so loudly!

Praise God; sing songs of praise.
Let others hear your confidence in God
and your gratitude for Jesus!

That is your testimony about the one who
loves us all beyond measure…

8

A Little Story...
Sittin' in the Café on a Sunday afternoon or two

As told by "A Fly on the Wall"

First Sunday:

Let's call this man George. His day began as a typical Sunday morning – coffee, newspaper and plans for lunch with his friends. Today, however, he took a slight detour on his journey...

"Hey fellas. How ya doin'? I just gotta tell ya I went to church this here mornin'. Yeah, yeah, get over it," he says, laughing, while pulling out his chair.

But as he sits, the tone changes. And with a sigh...

"And ya know, I got nothin out of it. That preacher isn't any good, or he musta been havin a bad day." *(Or, to paraphrase:*

I didn't enjoy myself, and it was entirely his fault! Doubt I'll ever be goin back there again.)

Second Sunday:

Those Sunday lunches must be a fixed routine because we find him in the same place one week later... running ever later than last week.

"Hey, fellas. Sorry I kept ya'll waitin'. I got outta church late today," he says with a grin. "Now don't you go laughin at me – thought I'd give it one more try cuz I ran outta coffee at home and there was a big pot of it in the lobby last week. Anyways...

"I went to church today; I sat down to say a little prayer – just to be polite, ya know – and then I lifted myself out o' the pew when they decided to sing a little praise. These bones are getting a little old, but I made it without embarassin' myself too awful much..."

After acknowledging the expressions of full understanding, he realizes another emotion has surfaced as well.

"And it wasn't just one time neither! Them folks was up and down so many times I wondered if I was gonna make it!

He continues, perhaps a little lost in thought,

"But somehow, it just got easier each time I did it! Pretty soon I found myself ready, willin' and able to stand...

"John, I see you smirkin'; wipe that grin off your face! Movin' on...

"Then I picked up that Bible in the back of the bench and opened it up only cuz someone sittin' next to me pointed out it's not enough just to hold it. Then that same person showed me how to turn to the Bible verse written on them big fancy screens at the front, and I got a paper cut! ...Nah, just addin a little drama to my story..." *he says with a grin.*

"Anyways, I held that open Bible in my lap until this lil' ol' lady next to me says, "It helps if you read it – the rest will make more sense if you do.

"I began to wonder if she's just lonely, or a regular, or if she actually wanted to help me...

"Back to that preacher. Next thing he does is start prayin' like nobody's business. Sometimes he sounded like a teacher; other times like he's cheerin' at a football game! Then he gets real quiet, ya now – so quiet I had to lean forward in my seat – oh well, one more exercise I can check off my list for the day," *he says with a little chuckle.*

Lowering his voice and leaning forward just a little he whispers,

"Anyways, then he gets real quiet and tells God he loves Him – that he's sorry for lettin' Him down, and that...now get this! He asks God to teach everyone how to love the people sittin' next to us the way Jesus does.

"I had to do it; I just couldn't resist. I open one eye just a tiny bit so as not to get caught, and I see that little ol' lady huggin her Bible, with a tear runnin' down her cheek. She musta seen me peekin, cuz she reaches over and pats my arm! I tell you, I had to close that eye o' mine mighty fast to prevent that tear in *my eye* from escapin!

"Now, Sam, don't you dare laugh at me!"

"And all the while, that preacher just keeps on a prayin'…

"Now he starts askin' God to forgive our sins. Hmmm, sounds like I'm not the only one in that category. I was afraid to turn around and look at the other folks, but decides to squeeze my eyes shut real, real tight cuz if that preacher catches me lookin' around he might think I am just as guilty as the next guy! No eye contact means innocence, right?

"Sure did seem like he'd a been praying a long time, and he musta been cuz all of sudden it's like it's already Valentine's Day! Goodness, time sure flies in that church; began to wonder if I needed a clean shirt…

"Anyways, the preacher missed all my confusion and just keeps on a tellin' God how much he loves Him. And, then he starts over again with that love stuff. I gotta tell ya, any card company could make a fortune if all their cards was written with his kinda love. Puppy dogs and big red hearts can't hold a candle to that kind –

"And then - he says Jesus taught him how to love like that!

"There she goes agin, that lil' ol' lady is pattin' my arm again – not like I'm in her way or nothin but just soft and lovin' like. Gotta admit it, fellas, I was beginning to enjoy that ol' gal," *he says with a smile.*

"But again, I'm not tellin' ya what I want to say. That preacher's prayer was just gettin things started. He tells us to read the Bible verses out loud, *like we mean it.* Well, gotta tell ya, that sounded a little judgmental to me, but I did it anyway. After a couple of words, I kinda notices I meant it more and more as I got close to that punkshiashun at the end of the sentence. Hmmm, I wonder if that would work at home?" *he says, cradling his chin in that scarred work hand of his.*

"Well, the point of my story is that by the time that preacher got thru explaining the Bible story, and that little ol' lady patted my arm so many times I lost count, I began to think that must be the best sermon I ever heard. To tell ya the truth, it might be the first one I really ever listened to! Do you reckon it is that way every time?

"Now don't laugh at me, you ol' codgers!

As the laughter begins to die out Bill looks each one in the eye, and says with only a slight hesitation in his voice,

"You guys reckon there's any more of them good verses left? If ya know one, I might even say one at home! But, have to admit, I would miss that lil' ol' lady pattin my arm though.

"Think I'll have to sit by her next Sunday too…"

9

~~~~~~~~~⌒⌒⌒~~~~~~~~~

Recognizin' Attitude can Make or Break Us

My Choice and God's Grace

And do not be conformed to this world,
but be transformed by the renewal of your mind,
that by testing you may discern what is the will of God,
what is good and acceptable and perfect
Romans 12:2 ESV

Would you like to join me (and that fly on the wall) to listen to the attitudes of others so often present in our days? It only takes a newscast, a blog, a magazine article, or even one conversation to learn the attitudes and ideas of others, doesn't it? Food for thought: what do the majority of us truly know about our own attitudes? Where do those prejudices - or identifications with our simple understanding of who we are becoming - actually begin? Can our own perceptions of life be frequently formed solely based on the attitudes of others?

Have you ever stopped to consider what *you* value? Does society 'plant' judgmental attitudes of life, religion, success, and people based on the values of others? And, do our minds then accept the attitudes of others as they blossom into the world's idea of truth? Or have you honestly considered what you – just you - understand as important or life changing or noteworthy? Do you ever seek a simple, quiet time to hear what God thinks about your life?

Do you spend more time finding out what others think than you do hearing God's opinions?

How often do you hear questions posed to friends or colleagues that end with 'Was I wrong for my attitude?' And then realize that the closer you listen, it becomes clear the question is asked not in an attempt to determine knowledge or identify a mistaken attitude, but to elicit a confirmation that one has acted in full justification? If there is truly a danger in wrong attitudes, then the sheer necessity of seeking truth from God is critical.

We live in a world that is trying its best to convince us that following the ideas and attitudes of others is our one greatest goal. If the desire is to be unique, to be the best you can be, to know and live truth, then one's best plan is to understand oneself better. How? Spend more time in prayer and Bible study to see and understand God's attitude, and Jesus' day-to day actions. Acknowledge that then, and only then, can one truly become all that God intended, thereby learning to accept both oneself and others. And beginning to understand your importance in this world…

Can you identify with the same struggles and attitude of the speaker in "Sittin' in a Café on a Sunday Afternoon" shared in the previous chapter? Think about it. It began with negatives. That first Sunday in church was not a pleasant experience for him, was it? Certainly, do note it did not take long for him to clarify the contributing factors to his negativity. Bottom line — church attendance failed his expectations *because it was someone else's fault.* And he immediately shared that frustration with others in the café. Why? Was it for the 'entertainment value?' I might say, partially. Do you think it could be genuine frustration, or an early protection policy against embarrassment if others found out he actually did attend church? Could it be either, or both?

The importance of the anecdote is the fact that he chose to go back to church the next Sunday. Was he looking for something, or Someone, but not sure exactly why he expected to find either one in church? Was it really the coffee, or was that just a defense prepared in advance in case the 'fellas' laughed at him? (Coffee drinkers, can you empathize? Church coffee just seems better.) He sounds like a good storyteller, and as such has that entertaining attitude as well as humorous input. *However, the key point is that he was still willing to try again.* For many that takes courage. For others it takes desperation. For still others it is the simple understanding that *encountering God is up to us as individuals.*

Did you follow the description of the person seated next to him, the one who prompted him to open that Bible he was holding? She was anonymous, unidentified at first. Did you stop to wonder why her identity was delayed? It is easy to overlook the powerful wisdom in the words as her role becomes 'one who suggests that opening it and reading the Bible offers more.' Could it be overlooked that this little lady's words had greater wisdom in that simple statement than others might have in long, drawn out monologues? Can you think of a better 'relationship' starter?

Have you ever been that person sitting by a newcomer? Do you make the most of every opportunity regardless of where it is presented? Or do you follow social niceties that cause some to hide their faith and witness even inside the church building? The weather is important, and knowing how that visitor came to be in your church that morning might be a polite segue into *later* conversation, but what if 'later' never comes?

Enough of wasted words, denied opportunities for salvation, and the countless distractions taking away from the wisdom one is there to learn and appreciate. Teach by your actions and God's truth always. Don't just rely on the preacher to teach truth – members have opportunities as well. Determine to do and say as God directs in every opportunity and every occasion and in every truth – in every pew and chair. There is a caution here, understand one's attitude is important as well. No oppression, or aggression, just love. 1 John 3:18 ESV says, "let us not love in word or talk but in deed and in truth." Be that little old lady or man! Be that teenager! Be that witness.

Be that witness that recognizes that the attitudes of others really do permeate our days. It is rare, however, for many to privately evaluate their own. It is common to share experiences – and our reaction to them with others. As you begin to listen to your words do you ever recognize the need to explain the positive merits of someone or something by contrasting it with just how awful it could have been? For so many, there is a temptation that exists when one wants to exemplify, celebrate or simply compliment someone or something by expressing a positive but then relies on subsequent negatives or criticisms, or identified faults to ensure the positive meaning is fully understood. That can then border on judgmental attitudes and it is a common means of communication. Conversely, individuals also use contrasting possibilities of good in their descriptions of bad - but in a world that trades on negatives how often do you even hear individuals discussing the good? Often, far too often, one criticizes the person whose efforts seem less experienced, less honest, or as one with questionable motives by vehemently describing how "it should have been." Far too often God is blamed for hardship created at the hand of compromised values, deserted loyalty to opportunities of learning more from the Bible, and mankind's failure to realize selfish desires.

**But once in a great while, the world
stops to listen, even if briefly,
to God and His mercy. And that is cause for jubilation!**

Oh, that jubilation shouldn't be so short-lived, and wouldn't it be wonderful to hear others praising God throughout the day, all day, and then let those who hear begin to speak and teach others? The severity of the criticisms and the extent of the jubilation over the positives are created by the attitude of the speaker. Choose Wisely.

In John Maxwell's book, *Attitude 101* from Thomas Nelson Publishers he describes Attitude as "the librarian of our past…the speaker of our present…and the prophet of our future." Consider the three metaphors used: librarians store and provide materials that present ideas, events and judgment on various topics; speakers tend to focus on information of merit that can, and often do, impact those listening, while the prophet makes predictions of events or attitudes that will present themselves in the future. Keep in mind that the future is often the result of, and impacted by, the actions of the present.

If you think about it, attitudes are usually an outward expression of the emotions one may or may not wish to keep hidden. Those emotions and attitudes are typically expressed through physical mannerisms or movements (throwing one's hands in the air in anger or condemnation is one good example; facial expressions are another, just to name a few.) Frequently, however, one's attitude makes its appearance as emotions "tumble out" in one's words or anger, frustration, or lack of understanding. Proverbs 15:13 ESV says, "A glad heart makes a cheerful face, but by sorrow of heart the spirit is crushed." How true. Now consider that 'lil' ol' lady – no name, just a woman who is known by her actions: how she hugged her Bible while a tear ran down her cheek as the preacher talked of loving God. And why would she reach over to pat the speaker's arm? Was it to scold him for looking at her tears or was it to show love for him too?

Notice how the speaker evaluates her motives early in the story – lonely, a regular, or if she actually wanted to help, but by the end he "begins to enjoy that ol' gal." Her attitude has won him over, taught him how to find the scripture, encouraged him, and changed his attitude simply by showing a caring spirit.

There is no more negativity about his first week in church; instead, there are new plans for the week ahead and the relationship with the truth of his Bible, and the lil' ol' lady loving him with each and every pat on his arm throughout the church service.

Wait! Now don't miss this part: After church he rushes to the Café, apologizing for arriving late and *desiring to share what he has seen and heard in church* - a story filled with conviction, friends, and humor. And he has already decided to enjoy God's blessing next week.

And with this I will close – he shared all he had learned. He did so by his actions, his enthusiasm, and his words as well as the smile on his face. That sounds like an example we could all follow don't you think?

By the way, that lil' ol' lady was never given a name... Could she have been you?

III.

**"Gladness" Implies
Purpose
You Can
Sing About**

God, what would You have me do today?
Giving, exercising, teaching,
living the very abilities God placed in me?

You determine how you will view the world.
Noah had a flood. God had a dove.
That place that may not be
Home Sweet Home…

10

―――❧❧❧――――

Good Morning, Lord!

It's a new day; it's a new dawn. It is a new beginning.

What if the first words that came out of our mouths each
day sounded something like this…?

Dear God, what is on *Your* mind today?
Yes, Lord, I will listen.
And, yes, I am interested! I promise.

Dear Jesus, what must I do to be saved?
John 3:16, for sure.
And how can I teach that to others?

**After that wonderful gift, what
must I do to be faithful?**
If I begin with being faithful to studying my Bible,
what do You, O God, have to teach me today?

**What must I learn to be able to live the
life you have given me today?**
Will you help me to understand my place in this world?

And then, what must I do as I enter my day?
Prayer seems like your first answer, but must it really be
with all my heart and soul and mind…?

**As I leave my place of prayer, what
would You have me do today?
It is your choice.**
Yes, Lord. I understand it really is Your choice…

11

Makin' a joyful noise...

**And allowing yourself to actually
feel and *enjoy the Joy*...**

Psalm 100:1-5 KJV

"Make a joyful noise unto the Lord, all ye lands.
Come before his presence with singing.
Know ye that the Lord he is God.
It is he that hath made us and not we ourselves.
We are his people, and the sheep of his pasture.
Enter into his gates with thanksgiving
and into his courts with praise.
For the Lord is good;
His mercy is everlasting;
and His truth endureth to all generations."

"Make a joyful noise unto the Lord all ye lands." Psalm 100:1 KJV

Remember that the "Earth is the Lord's and the fullness thereof..." Psalm 24:1 ESV. Nature is not only God's gift to us, but it is also God's message of beauty and provision. Daily it is a witness to the miracles and glory of God. It is not man-made; it is rarely controlled by even man's best efforts. It is God's. Perhaps this verse is both reference to, and acknowledgement of who Nature truly belongs to and the gratitude that should be shown. Are we to give the birds a new song to sing, or will we allow them to be all God created them to be? Are we to take the sustenance provided for granted? Are we treasure it, or cover it up?

Human beings do have a role to play in the earth's protection. First of all, it is up to us to be respectful of *all* God created – and among His creation are those people in our sphere of influence. "All ye lands" means everything you or I own, influence, take part in, and work for and live in and live with. Those are our "lands," and we have an obligation to celebrate God in them and lead others to do the same. It is not an obligation we enter into begrudgingly but one we must embrace with love and excitement and joy.

How exactly do we do that? Always take that first step carefully. *Stop and recognize God as the Creator.* Show respect for Him. Take the time to know Him – through prayer that constitutes and develops a personal relationship; read the Bible to learn the history of God and His interaction with people throughout time. See His blessings; understand that His discipline is a means of teaching mankind a better way than the one they insisted upon choosing for themselves. Pay close attention to His willingness to forgive and love without measure. Encouraging others to do the same is your way to ensure all your "lands" are joyous in their praise of God. You be the example.

Stop and Recognize God as the Creator
Show Respect for Him
Take the time to know Him
Read your Bible to learn about Him
See His Blessings

Pay close attention to His willingness to
forgive and love without measure.

Now, take a moment to consider all "your lands." Write them below as a reminder to pray over them regularly – and pray for understanding of your role within those lands.

"Come before his presence with
singing." Psalm 100:2 KJV

Have you ever stopped to ask why people sing? Some songs are happy; some are sad. There are the ones sung on a birthday. Love songs. Songs of remembrance. Songs of rebellion. Songs of silliness. But, are those also songs of awareness? Does the music itself communicate ideas we struggle to simply say to another?

Music has long been used to soothe our souls, to focus our efforts as in the trumpet that leads the way into battle, to ignite passions within our being to love, to lead, to march forward, and to praise. Have you ever wondered why music is the introductory element in many of the world's worship services? Perhaps it is to involve the congregation in the service from the very beginning.

Music invites all to participate in the praise, to stand, to hear the words sung about God and Jesus, and about life as they know it. As they live it.

For some, Praise and Worship music encourages them to get on their feet, perhaps wave their hands toward Heaven, eyes closed and hearts open. Many of the words are repeated to ensure learning, and the rhythm makes the true application of the words evident to the very beating of our hearts, while the notes build to importance, and humility is sung in whispers of love.

It is as if the music prepares us to genuinely learn from the pastor and begin to see the application of scripture in our daily lives. There is renewed motivation to understand and to be actively engaged with the application of scripture – the same scripture that was just sung about.

Are those last two paragraphs the reasons we sing in churches? Yes. And oftentimes, the atmosphere created in the music develops a desire to hear more of the One we worship. Then, the excitement of hearing God's Word and applying it to our own lives, and even taking notes to insure we do not forget what we have learned becomes the foundation of singing praises regardless of where we are. In the car, as we go about our daily tasks, as we soothe ourselves and those around us…

The words become a part of our conversations.
The praise becomes a part of our prayers.
And God is glorified.

That is why we sing – regardless of the quality of our voices, regardless of needing to hum a few phrases because we forgot the words, regardless of where we are or who we are with.

We choose to praise God because He deserves to hear it – regardless of our singing ability. He hears the sound our heartstrings. And He loves it!

"Know ye that the Lord he is God. It is he that hath made us and not we ourselves.
we are his people, and the sheep of
his pasture." Ps 100:3 KJV

Do you realize how very special you are to God? He could have created you any one of a million ways or more. Yet, He made you the unique and wonderful person you are. There is no design flaw in your soul. Far too often society attempts to make us feel there are flaws in our physical bodies, in our intelligence, in our abilities, but that is a lie. Plain and simple. God knew what He was doing; He selected each and every part of You with love and purpose. Please know and appreciate that. Even if you have to remind yourself of that fact on a minute-by-minute basis. Even if you struggle with your self-image. God did not make a mistake. Enjoy the miracle of who you are and allow yourself to live in it daily.

I suppose being a high school teacher reminded me of those typical insecurities of teen years as I watched the students' needs to be accepted or respected or "equal" to others. And I saw the heartbreak as the price many paid destroyed their self-worth. For me, it turns out I was unique for God's purpose, even if I did not understand it then. And I didn't, believe me. Will you take a moment to think back to your teenage years…were you a carbon copy of every other person in your school? Did you want to be? Or were you the ideal model who may or may not have been miserable inside? It is typical for individuals to judge themselves based on the image of others…and to accept that one is different can be difficult.

However, God is still God, and He chose you to
be unique. He loves you just as you are.
If you remember no more than that, and if you would only
thank Him for all He has provided, then this book has been
what it is intended to be. I truly want you to know that.

He allowed you to be who you are for a purpose – a purpose often not realized until later in life, but none the less valuable! He has always had a plan for your life – a life that is loved, whose God-given ideas can benefit others, provide for them, and teach others about the respect God deserves. He planned for your happiness, for the forgiveness of any and all mistakes, and for your life to make a difference in this world. God has always had the perfect plan, but evil has never wanted you to know that. It wants you to suffer from confusion, from anger, from questioning your worth. Or doubting God. Choose to deny evil that opportunity. Just Choose.

Know that you know that you know God is real. Accept this. Refuse the fear or the pride that says mankind knows a better way. Refuse the rewritten laws of human existence, God's purpose, God's superiority. Refuse to worship the egotistical, the material, the words or actions that diminish the purpose of God. Give credit where credit is due and tell others about the real God. And Thank Him for the opportunity you have been given to do so!

One last thing that must be included here is the reference to being the sheep, the ones protected through starlit nights as they graze and relax in the music of the Shepherd's lyre. Understand the protection for the ones who have been, are being, or are now longing for the quick rescue from the danger of predators. The Shepherd never leaves His sheep. He is always there. Present. Protective. Powerful.

Acknowledge that sheep are not necessarily dumb, as many try to say. But, they are followers. Please choose wisely whose plan you are following. Perhaps that wording is God's way of reminding you that you are given the choice to follow evil and its ways, or you have the power to choose God's way, God's love, God's perfect plan for your life and thereby know the true joy that exists in a relationship with Him. And then, joyously say thank you for all the wonderful things a godly life can accomplish in this world.

"Enter into his gates with thanksgiving and into his courts with praise." Ps 100:4 KJV

You may say, "We just talked about that," but consider the further application of that verse. Gratitude. Saying "Thank You" often. *Choosing to open any gate that could possibly separate us from God.* Determining that you will allow nothing to separate you from His presence while becoming more and more and more aware of how present God always is in our lives - in every moment, every joy, every struggle - while offering yet another opportunity to openly state that *"every good and perfect gift is from above, coming down from the Father of heavenly lights, who does not change."* James 1:17 NIV. God is God. Jesus is Jesus. The plan for you and for this world does not change with each new wind of "man-made doctrine," or each outburst of emotion, or new leader who appears on the world scene. Mankind is given the freedom of choice, but not all choices are beneficial to our lives. Only by understanding that all honor must be given to God can we ever hope to find the very things that human beings are seeking.

That deserves gratitude and prayer to ensure each gift is used wisely and in accordance with the perfect plans God has for your life and the lives of others.

"For the Lord *is* good; his mercy *is* everlasting,
and his truth *endureth* to all generations."
Psalm 100:5 KJV

You know, I think that last verse says it all… That fact, written deliberately in your Bible, spoken by one who truly knew God, and offered to you on this day is there for a reason. It is there to make you feel confident, secure and loved by One who will never leave you. It is probably one of the greatest facts ever written…please don't forget it.

"You make known to me the path of life;
In Your presence there is fullness of joy;
At your right hand are pleasures forevermore."
Psalm 16:11 ESV

12

---·❦·---

Serving Sounds
like Work...

Gladness Implies Purpose You Can Sing About

*"Serve the Lord with gladness: Come
before His presence with singing."*
Psalm 100:2 KJV

Raise your hand if you would enjoy a simple day of joy, of
being loved, of attempting something great – and succeeding.
What would you have on your schedule? Reading, art,
conversation with friends or family, a day in the sunshine,
rest? Think about that for a moment...

I think sometimes we all forget that each and every one
of those things are made available every single day of our
lives. Oh, maybe not sunshine every day, but rain can be
soothing as well. There truly can be a perfect day; we simply
must allow God to create it.

I look back at the list of activities listed above and wonder why we often think those perfect days are unavailable to us. Life takes work, and that may be tiring, but at the end of the day we have the privilege of knowing we accomplished something. The "great or not" is up to us.

Feeling you are loved creates that warm, confident, secure feeling, right? However, there will be times that the love of others seems to be fickle. The love you give does not have to be – there is joy is knowing you have shown genuine love to someone, anyone, those who need it most. Do you ever find yourself wishing for someone who welcomes honest conversation without being judgmental, angry, or unwilling to simply sit and listen? There is. Know that you know that you know for every struggle we face there will always be an alternative to defeat, despair or total destruction. If you want to acknowledge it.

That alternative is God.

We must *allow* ourselves to feel the joy, the gladness, the pleasure in a personal relationship with God. He is mighty; He is powerful; He is Supreme, and He is your Friend. And true, loving friendships need to be celebrated. And honored. And always growing, developing and maturing.

Psalm 100:2 KJV says "Serve the Lord with gladness…" How better to understand the concept of gladness than to see it from God's context? As ever, it is important to take the time to consider the full meaning of the words used in your Bible.

Serving God, living the qualities of love, and giving of oneself to a greater purpose promotes and results in gladness. In you, and in those around you. Knowing you have done as

God asked is actually quite thrilling. It is not oppression or drudgery. It is living life above and beyond any negativity or rebellion. It is instilling joy, long-lasting joy in those around you. It opens the door of truth for many who might never hear of God or Jesus - simply by your excitement about your faith.

Serving the Lord is actually serving
(giving, exercising, teaching, living)
with the gifts God has already given you.

It is your opportunity to give back to God *the very abilities God placed in each of us.* In you. If willing to use those gifts with His guidance, mercy, grace, and as a part of the plans God had for our individual lives long ago – yet needed today – you find a gladness, a joy you could only imagine on your own. There is a joy in knowing your life has a purpose. It is feeling each day of your life has meaning. It also creates a greater awareness of God's presence throughout each day as the Holy Spirit touches your arm to remind you are called for "such a time as this." Read the story of Esther in Chapter 4 in of the book of Esther in your Bible. God provided an answer to His people; He guided Esther's life to be in the right place at the right time to provide that answer; He used Mordecai to remind Esther that she had a valuable opportunity – that perhaps her entire life was preparation for this moment in time. God provided the strength needed, the encouragement to work through the fear, and the confidence that God wanted to use her life to accomplish His will. With that example, how can any of us argue with God about our ability to serve others?

On the other hand, misery can and will be draining. Misery takes the focus off of "every good and perfect gift," from God. James 1:17 KJV. And instead focuses on every miserable event or potential event, every dissatisfaction, every unrealized goal – simply because one refuses to look for any reason to feel joy. It can quickly become a crutch, a desire for others to take responsibility for your happiness, or an open door to destruction of all that one holds dear. This is not a reference to mental illness; it is the ongoing choice to be miserable because it has become familiar. Maybe it is a true denial of God and all that He has said, He desires and offers to each of us. Maybe it is the desire to blame God for unfortunate events in life. I realize "unfortunate" is inadequate to describe abuse or neglect or hatred, but those things are not of God. All will live with consequences of others, but those "others" are not God. God always has a better way for today, regardless of yesterday. It is up to us to begin looking for the goodness, the gladness of a relationship with God, the opportunity to use our pasts to reach out to others who also need to realize there is a place for joy.

That place is with God.

One point is necessary to include here: Serving the Lord with gladness means enthusiasm for God. About God. Your experiences may genuinely provide an opportunity to encourage others struggling with the same sorrows. However, recognize that people who are miserable have no interest in one more person giving them one more reason to be miserable. You cannot help others find joy if you continually choose to live in your misery. You cannot share hope for a brighter future if you refuse to see your future living with the love and joy of God. You cannot teach gladness or joy if you do not understand it yourself. And you cannot understand it without God.

God is a gracious God, and I do not believe He would ever want hardship to fall on any of us. Evil is the source of abuse, neglect, hurt, etc. God is the source of strength, comfort and joy. Use your hurt to comfort others by teaching them about God's type of love. You feel their pain – help to heal it knowing, for yourself, how important God is to living a life that makes one want to wake up in the morning. Use your experience as the motivation to invite others to feel the joy that God provides. Use that motivation in your own spirit, and then take it to others with the testimony that God really does mean what He says in our Bible.

Understand that the lasting joy isn't like happiness which is based upon events or whether things are going well or not. No, joy remains even in the midst the suffering. Joy is not fleeting happiness. Joy is an emotion that **requires a Choice** to see God in the midst of circumstances. Where God is there is joy. **Anticipate** His Presence, knowing you are never alone. **Expect** something great or wonderful, **because God is great and wonderful**.

We must *allow* ourselves to feel the joy, the gladness, the pleasure in a personal relationship with God. He is mighty; He is powerful; He is Supreme, and He is your Friend. And true, loving friendships need to be celebrated and enjoyed.

And Gratitude must be expressed.

Tina Wash

My flesh and my heart may fail, but God is the strength of my heart and my portion forever." Psalms 73:26 NIV

A Simple Prayer for your day…

It is one I have prayed for you, the
reader, whoever you may be.
It is one that I have prayed for myself as well –
Many, many times!

"Dear Lord Jesus,
I pray I will be still long enough to hear You
And wise enough to understand not only Your words
but their application to my life.
Those must be my priority,
And those will undoubtedly be my blessings.
Undoubtedly.
Thank You, Lord."

13

———— ◦/◦/◦ ————

Singin' Solo

Sing to the best of your ability — and remember you
"can do all things through Christ who strengthens" you.
Philippians 4:13

Start with *Fact Number One*: Evil wants you to think it is you against the world, and evil will attempt to discourage you from stepping out and sharing your faith. It will attempt to frustrate or anger you; it will encourage indifference to the things of God. It will rob you of your joy when you least expect it. Please understand your joy is not dependent on others, on groups, on circumstances. I understand you may question that statement, but joy, real joy, is entirely your choice, and is freely available from Jesus.

It is up to you to determine how
you will view the world.
You determine how you will praise God.
You determine if you even will.
It is your choice. But God is still there, regardless.

Fact Number Two: Joy, deep abiding joy is not fleeting. Happiness may come and go, but joy never leaves…if you have chosen the One who provides that joy regardless of circumstances, emotions, finances, fear.

Life may put us in situations we never imagined, but God is still there. In hardship, in loss, in stress, in the inability to care for ourselves or others. But God is still there, attempting to capture your attention, determined to care and love and teach you that your future still exists in Him. Because God will still be there.

You may be singing in a big group right now, but sometimes we have to do it alone. We have to reach deep down inside us and remember who God is. And then trust His Will for our lives. There will be times others cannot sing, so it is up to you to do it for others, for God. Feel the hope He provides; demonstrate and teach that hope to others.

When life gives difficulty, the natural tendency is to crawl under the covers, hide your head and wish for better days. And yet…

The sun still shines.
The birds still sing.
The wind still whistles
And The horns still honk.

Sometimes you just "gotta stand" in the cold and sing. For your own encouragement and for others. Psalm 40:3 ESV says, "He put a new song in my mouth, a song of praise to our God. Many will see and fear and put their trust in the Lord." Well! It seems to me the best response to that is a hearty and sincere, "Thank You!"

Two additional points I really want to make at this point. Note the use of the pronoun, "my." God gives the song *to you*. God gives the hope *to you*. And God appreciates the praise *from you*. That is your witness. Help others understand that "fear" in these verses is not associated with being afraid. Fear is respect – for the One who is greater, mightier, wiser, and more loving than we could ever be. It is giving honor and understanding that a lack of respect for God becomes the source of all misery and doubt and fear and confusion.

Fact Number Three. Attempts to gain needed knowledge require choice. It takes mental strength and physical effort to pick up a book or the Bible. It takes faith to pray even when the needed conversation with God makes you fear He might not listen. Or, you fear He might answer. And yet, He always listens, and He always has an answer whether we choose to listen or not. It takes courage to join others in Bible Study, especially when one lacks the same spiritual background. And, in all three instances – study, prayer, and fellowship with other Christians - those are the ways you will gain experience with the knowledge of God. Choose to act. And before you may even realize it you will begin seeing God's wisdom leading your life in ways you never imagined!

Strength and power and knowledge are by-products of choosing to learn. That three-fold combination can lead and guide one's choices. But never forget that Spiritual guidance is from God and often spoken simply and quietly by the Holy Spirit. Stop and Listen. That ensures the wisdom needed to live a life worthy of one's calling. God will always be nearby cheering you on. However, you must choose the willingness to obey. It is your choice, but one must choose wisely. The understanding earned is God's gift and should certainly be recognized as such.

But, where does one go to learn? How does one live a life devoted to learning about God? How can you be sure you are finding truth? Why is this learning "assignment" so important? I offer three helpful guidelines:

#1 – Always study the Bible and spend time in prayer.
#2 – Always recognize God is present,
     and no truth will ever contradict God.
#3 – Always Focus on God to know what tidbits
     He needs to emphasize that day,
     in your life and the lives of others.

Simple list. Sometimes difficult choices. However, we grow by challenging ourselves. The reason you *will* find what you are looking for is because God is always waiting on you to live a life that actually waits on Him so that you will become the absolute best version of yourself! Fact: waiting for anything seems the hardest thing we are faced with on a daily basis! Yes, it is a challenge to rearrange schedules to spend time in Bible Study and Prayer. But it is worth every minute. It may be a challenge to let go of the negativity you are faced with on a daily basis, but is that resulting suffering what you had hoped for? I could continue on with my list, but I simply want you to find what your heart is looking for – love, peace, knowing you are a person of worth, and recognizing God sees you as His treasure. Yes, there will be struggles, but what a joy it is to know Jesus is on your side if you will only allow Him to be.

Psalm 46:10 NIV says, "Be still and know" that He is God. Stop resenting the guidelines included in your Bible; stop trying to re-write the Bible to fit your plans. God enabled the writing of that text thousands of years ago specifically for our benefit– it has not lost its relevance nor will it ever have a need to be rewritten. If you have not realized its importance spend more time studying it, and then sit back and marvel at how often you recognize your life, your struggles and the depth of your joys written on the very pages of the Bible. "Hear" the words that contain specific wisdom or understanding for the very life you are living!

Enter any bookstore and find books of devotions written by Christian authors and share in their understanding. Find a church that will teach you more. Relish the fellowship that will encourage you – do not demand all be perfect but learn from their examples, give of yourself and your gifts to bless others, and celebrate the life applications of scripture. Know that all are applicable to today, to your life, to the world.

I know it may be hard at first; it is permissible to complain about the challenges, but you deserve the chance to see that all will never be lost. This world will never defeat those whose faith is based on Jesus.

14

"Into each life a little
rain must fall."

From "The Rainy Day"
By Henry Wadsworth Longfellow

*"The Lord your God is in your midst, a mighty one who will
save; He will rejoice over you with gladness; He will quiet
you by His love; He will exult over you with loud singing."*
Zephaniah 3:17 ESV

Noah had a flood, and God had a dove. My hometown also
had a flood of epic proportions for West Texas. And God
had a Deacon.

After heavy rains throughout the night streets were
filled with deep, deep currents flowing quickly to the main
thoroughfares. Our concerns that Sunday morning were
great. Unaware of the dangers, many still fought their way to
that 8:15 am service. Understandably, our minds were a little

distracted as the service began, and almost all worried about the streets we would need to navigate on the way home.

Yet, we had survived the "voyage" to church! And we were there to learn…and M.B. Carrell was there to teach. He was not a Bible Study teacher; he was not the preacher. He had no massive Bible in his hand to administer justice to the children running in the hallways. (I say that in jest – no one could have been kinder.)

His job that morning was to pray. And he did so in a way that has remained in my heart to this day. Mr. Carrell spoke to God in a way that acknowledged quickly all God is and *all He had already done that morning.* As we sat there still damp from the heavy rain, with shoes placed neatly beside our wet feet to allow both to dry, his prayer began with, "Lord, thank you for the sunshine!"

Audible gasps filled the Sanctuary. Eyes flew open and hearts beat a little faster in concern for his health in that moment. People needed to see that Mr. Carrell was okay. As a man respected in that church the concern was immediate and palpable…and then he continued, "because even if it is raining, we know the sun is still shining just behind the clouds. Your Son is still shining." The concerns were diminished. The fear was replaced with thoughtful joy. Focus was moved from the dramatic rain event to God - who was still in control, who was still encouraging us through the prayers of one individual. Faith was strengthened. The gratitude for a lesson well-taught brought smiles all around, a few chuckles, and the wisdom still remains.

I want you to consider the depth of faith that allows one to see the chaos, the hurt, the struggle and still confidently say, "Thank You, God. I know you are still here." The key word in the chapter title is "MUST." It truly is the wise among us who accept that sadness will come at some point or another, but the joy of Jesus, of a life lived for Him will far, far outweigh the sadness – if you let it. If you choose it. If you trust the source of that joy; let me rephrase that, if you choose Jesus and allow Him to offer what He came to earth to offer: love, forgiveness, hope, teaching, strength, and joy.

Forgive me, but I tend to play with words and phrases I want to remember, and my typical memorization tool is to create an acrostic in which each letter represents further information to be remembered. Here goes!

In times of flooding (of emotion, hurt, confusion or doubt) consider the following:

F	**Faith**	…gotta have it!
		Hebrews 11:1 NIV. *'Now **faith** is the substance of things hoped for, the **evidence** of things not seen"*
L	**Location**	…in the arms of God
		Deuteronomy 30:20 NIV. *"listen to His voice. and hold fast to him."*
O	**Opportunity**	Look for the lesson or opportunity contained within the problem.
		Proverbs 4:25 NIV. *"Let your eyes look straight ahead…"* Quit reliving the struggle, instead see the protection, the lessons, the hope provided by God.

O   Open   Remain open to God's presence and His purpose.

Ephesians 1:17-18 ESV. That God "may give you a spirit of wisdom and of revelation [understanding] in the knowledge of Him, having your hearts enlightened, that you may know the hope to which He has called you…" Read that carefully – He has already planned for you to see the hope, the light at the end of the tunnel - what He needs is for you to join Him in the conversation and experience the love that makes your hope possible.

D   Determination   Choose to trust God no matter what!!!

Psalm 121:5 NIV. "The Lord watches over you…" Never will His eyes turn away.

The simple fact of life is that everyone will experience difficulty and heartache at some point: Tears of hurt or of loss or just simple sadness, but everyone can also know Tears of Joy, Tears of Cleansing, Life-giving Tears, and Tears that accompany Growth from Lessons Learned. Tears of any kind can be healthy if one allows them to be - *while keeping one eye on God.*

The question all of us need to ask in times of struggle is: "Am I allowing God's beauty to grow in His sunshine during this time of rain?" Remember Mr. Carrell. "Thank you for the sunshine, because even though we cannot see it right now, **we know it is just behind the clouds.**"

15

Headin' Home

To that place that may not be "Home Sweet Home"

Environment, Attitude, Choices

We are each a product of our environment, whether we want to be or not. Because that is so, it appears we must then ask ourselves, "Do I want my environment to control, model, predict who I am and who I will become?" If so, remain in an awareness of your needs. If not, you have the opportunity to make a change.

The first thought for many is "I can't change my environment." That may very well be true – but only in the physical sense. Income, family, education, and societal systems seem to both control and guide who many are, who they desire to be, and who they are ultimately willing to choose to be.

Unfortunately, the physical surroundings cannot often be changed. Family, for better or worse, often seems to determine our outlook, our location, our safety or the love we feel from others. But! One is never doomed to a future that is hopeless, lost, defeated, unloved or uneducated. Those factors are often a choice. Please, do not react solely to that last statement. Hardships are reality and seem to control one's outlook and/or motivation to make a better life. Thankfully, there is One who has the ability, the desire, the hope and certainly the power to provide each and every one of us a life that has hope and love and purpose, regardless of our physical circumstances. That One is Jesus. And He is living inside each and every one of us. He sees tomorrow; He sees our worth; He sees the child inside us dreaming of hope.

Physical realities may exist, and they may endure, but the spirit within each of us has the choice to see the world in a different light, to feel joy in our soul, to know that help is only a prayer away. No one can truly control our minds. No one can truly control our heart's desire. No one can take away your hope unless you choose to allow that.

> **"Jesus came that we might have life, and that
> we might have it more abundantly."
> John 10:10.
> Jesus loves you. Period.
> Yes, your circumstances may break His
> heart, but they do not predict
> who you are, who you can be, and who God
> loves with an eternal, unselfish love.**

Without a glimpse of the joy that is possible through Jesus, this may seem a fantasy. Hope for the future? Unselfish love? You may not even understand those concepts, but you have the opportunity to do so, and no one can take that opportunity away from you. Many have chosen to participate in a faith that tends to be exuberant, filled with beauty and grace, and a faith that is real. And you are invited to do the same. God is real. Jesus truly is the Son of God who came to earth to live as a man and teach there is a better way to live our lives – regardless of circumstances.

Read the stories of the sick, blind, and the lame who came to Jesus for healing as told in Matthew, Mark, Luke and John in your Bible. Be amazed by the events containing hungry people who were fed miraculously on a hilltop; and know they were there because even hunger could not discourage their desires to hear Jesus' teaching. Dip your finger into the waters as Jesus did, and imagine the power of His ability to heal those in need at the Pool of Bethesda in John 5. Imagine the blind beggar calling out to Jesus and knowing Jesus alone had the power to heal him. His faith is evident as he addresses Jesus as the Son of God. In return, he experienced One who was willing to take the time to heal him, to encourage hope. Mark 10:46-52.

Imagine the trust, loyalty and friendship of the disciples who chose to leave their lives, without question, to follow Him as He taught and ministered, despite others who opposed Jesus' ministry. See the children around you and love them as Jesus loved. In fact, you are invited to be among the children Jesus loved and welcomed despite busy days and weariness. Matthew 19:14.

You have the opportunity to learn more about God and Jesus if you will only take the time to read more in the Bible. If you have a Bible, read it. If you don't, all is not lost. Go to others who can teach you. You may even utter a simple prayer and ask for knowledge. Know that God can use even the most awkward prayer to speak to your heart.

Turn your eyes away from the anger and hatred so prevalent in this world and seek the love that is offered freely, without manipulation, with concern for your good - not your destruction. Raise your eyes, straighten your back, and pray for help, for understanding, for mercy, and for joy. Know that the only one who truly has the ability to hear your prayers is God. Recognize that He alone has the power and compassion to understand your heart. Choose to believe that Jesus was sent to this world for you, that His love is pure, and only He can prevent eternal damnation. Choose to believe. The choice is yours, and while the world may seek to take away your choices – no one can take away your choice to believe in Jesus and the salvation that only He can offer.

Psalm 33 encourages us all to respect and recognize God's great majesty and know the unique characteristics of God. No human being can ever provide the power that God can. And none can replace Him. Read Psalm 33: 16 - 22 NIV *aloud right now.* Hear the truth, understand God alone offers truth, recognize that only Jesus can save, and let your heart be filled with His joy. How? Trust in Him.

One more verse in that chapter I want you to consider, "Let your steadfast love, O Lord, be upon us even as we hope in You." Psalm 33:27 NIV. AS we hope, not only *while we hope but to the degree we trust in God.* HOW we hope is critical – do so with confidence in who He is and discipline for who we are as human beings prone to doubt and distraction, (Yes, that is one aspect of life that we cannot deny). Praise God for who He is and how much He loves you.

As always, asking a favor of anyone carries with it an obligation to say, "Thank You." Those words of gratitude often take the form of praise – recognizing and worshipping Him as well as letting others know of the miraculous kindness of God. Know God and Praise Him without end... and never forget to audibly say, "Thank You, Lord."

One important caution: If you and I are not choosing to be fully aware of God's Presence every minute of every day, and if we refuse to communicate with God about our circumstances, our Hope can look, sound and be hopeless, and if we fail to say "Thank You, we could easily return to that state of mind that accepts defeat and discouragement, that sees our hardships rather than His hope, and simply chooses to exist rather than live.

Will you see your life immediately change to one of joy? Yes, because joy is already inside you, just waiting to be acknowledged. It is an emotion we choose. Will you begin to feel that pure, unselfish love regardless of circumstances? It is up to you. But the opportunity is certainly available! Romans 15:13 NIV is the invitation...

IV.

Okay,
Mountain,
Here I Come!

Playin' the Games of Life

God Has A Vision for Your Life

Never forget!
The Reward is at the Top -
The Dissatisfaction is at the Bottom.

Let the Shoutin' Begin!
No Fear, Just Pure Unadulterated Joy!

16

～∾～

Playin' the Games Of Life

Of Desires and Guarantees...

Now consider the "What if" game? Fanciful dreams of success, of treasures desired, of items needed but not guaranteed at the time due to finances, schedules, priorities. "What if" soon becomes a case of stating our desires and expecting another to guarantee that our requests are honored.

> "What if I give you my teddy bear," will you promise to give it back in two minutes? If we traded ownership of a video game, would you let me choose the one **I** want?
> "What if" I said I love you, would you promise to love me too?
> "What if" I offered to pay you back later would you give me what I need/want right now? (And then find that "right now" often leads on to "Oh, next week" or "I

95

just can't do that right now" or even "I don't remember promising you *that*!")

Isn't "What If…" actually the same game people play with relationships, credit cards, home mortgages, new cars? **With promises to God?** "What if" I make that profession of faith in Jesus would that guarantee all my troubles would end? "What if" I said, "I Love You, Lord," would you really, really love me the way the Bible says, or *the way I want to be loved*?" Understand the ways we want to be loved do not always agree with the character or teachings of Jesus,

"What if" I follow my own path today, will you still wait for me at the end of the road?

Note: the "what ifs," stated or implied, beginning each statement are not really promises to do *anything*. They do not denote a commitment already made and/or a guaranteed willingness to keep one's part of the bargain. Each is simply the desire to have another's guarantee that the resulting action would be the benefit desired.

Have you heard others playing the same games? And it is a game – one attempting to have desires met but only if he or she gets to control the outcome. Now take time to consider an even bigger question, have you ever heard Jesus playing that game? Or God? No.

"You will seek me and find me, when you seek me with all your heart."
Jeremiah 29:13 ESV

Stop and consider how many times, as a child, you played the game, "Hide and Seek." Remember the excitement, the determination to find your friend when you were "it"? Remember the feelings of frustration – even abandonment – when you found the perfect hiding place - only to feel sorrow because you were left alone when you could not be found? However, let me repeat…

> *"You will seek me and find me, when*
> *you seek me with all your heart."*
> Jeremiah 29:13 ESV

In other words, God does not choose to hide from those who seek Him. Period – so is that comma a warning sign for the reader? The fact that the comma is present is important –there is more clarification to be recognized. Is the rest of the sentence crucial to the truth of the first part?

Sooner or later, we will all go looking for God simply because we recognize the need for more than this world could or would ever offer. Someday all will wake up and become frightened or dissatisfied or confused, or simply realize that our world has lost its way. We as individuals have lost our way. But, God has not.

God does not demand you offer Him a life of perfection in exchange for the Salvation offered through Jesus. Take a minute to truly consider that, then look back at your life and determine if you have lived a perfect life *in any area* simply because Jesus offered you the forgiveness of sin. Did God provide the guidance in the Bible seeking a guarantee you would learn it and follow it and appreciate it? Have you seen Him withdraw it because you refuse to read it?

If any of those questions seem to demand too much 'reality' or truth are you willing to join the millions who are believing in the one true God? The One who offers each and "every perfect gift" while at the same time attempting to strengthen your dedication to the **commitment God made long ago**: To allow Jesus to suffer for your sake. To provide actual applications to life as we know it so that we might understand. To allow you to hold tightly to Him – while often dragging your feet - as He teaches the difficult lessons. And the appreciation? The Joy? The Faith? Is it evident in your life?

In truth, the "what if" has been omitted, and God simply says, "I want you to have this, no matter what." Will that put an end to your desire for control? Will you learn to trust? Will you allow yourself to see the joy in all circumstances? Will you choose to believe in a Savior who never has, and never will play games with the Salvation He offers to all who believe?

> *"Let me hear what God the Lord will speak, for*
> *He will speak peace to His saints,*
> *But let them not turn back to folly.*
> Psalm 85:8-9 ESV

17

Singin' in the Valley

*"As for me, I am poor and needy, but
the Lord takes thought for me..
You are my help and my Deliverer…"*
Psalm 40:17 ESV

God has a vision for your life, and as much as many of us would like to say we are fully qualified to make Him proud, we are not. One's life can typically contain streams of living water, pastures of rest, mountaintops of excitement and joy, and an occasional valley along the journey. We may very well find ourselves in a valley of need, but that does not mean that same valley is not filled to overflowing with a beauty that often surprises us. God is love, and our journey will always be filled with God's mercy and peace and strength – and that is the beauty available to us if we only seek Him.

The part I love is that God never loses His vision for you, and for me. He just continues to mold our lives and encourage our growing maturity in our responses until we are ready to actually do as he commands, intends, or simply desires so that we can become a part of His magnificent plan.

Oswald Chambers stated this way:

> *"God gives us a vision, and then He takes us down to the valley... It is in the valley that so many of us give up and faint. Every God-given vision will become real if we will only have patience...He has to take us to the valley and puts us through fires and floods to batter us into shape, until we get to the point where He can trust us with the reality of the vision."*

Life is good, and God is great. That statement alone could be this entire chapter.

However, as in so much of the human life we sometimes forget the simple truths of God. Those are the times we question, we fear, we do not understand, and those are the times our circumstances attempt to rule our emotions. Then, in that never-ending path of doubt or self-destruction, the emotions can then begin to rule our thoughts, and we are in danger of losing our joy.

Gone is the exhilaration of seeing God at work. Missing is the excitement to begin a new endeavor or a new day with God. Absent is the calm understanding needed in the midst of hurt or confusion.

"Then" is the cause and effect of life as we know it. If and Then. Ignoring the fact that life is good, regardless, because God is good might lead one to...Giving up before crossing God's Finish Line due to fatigue or injury. Choosing to fail or doubt, because some days life is just plain hard. Allowing the thoughts of others to crowd out the thoughts of God rather than honoring our wonderful gift of understanding. Remember, God is always in control. God always has a better way. God can use anyone and anything to accomplish good for His Kingdom. May I repeat? God is always in control.

It takes a strong individual to fight life's battles, and if you are like most, strength tends to come and go. Faith remains and God remains, but the strength can become fleeting.

Will you join me in taking one deep breath right now?

Breathe in the presence of One who loves you.
Count to 10.
Pray for understanding.
If you created a problem, confess that
and seek guidance; then act.
If you didn't seek to understand what you
are to focus on, what you are to learn,
and how to praise throughout, then listen now.
Recognize there is still beauty in the valleys of life.

Close your eyes. Hear the small stream as it trickles through the rocks and then becomes a rapid as it clears the obstructions. Feel the joy of freedom in the rushing waters. Let yourself feel the beginnings of excitement and continue on.

Follow the winding path of the stream. Marvel at the peaceful, gentle flow of life – once the struggle in the rocks is passed. See the quiet stillness where fish gather to feed on "food" that has been washed downstream to nourish and grow – that is your time with God; it is your guidance provided by the Bible. It is where you begin saying "Thank You" as you learn, reflect and praise.

Turn your gaze to the sky. See the glory of God. Note the sparrows flying above and remember God has His eye on them as well. And appreciate the fact that trees are already provided so that they may rest when weary. Can you hear their songs of joy as they nestle among the leaves moving softly in the breeze?

Turn to see God's creatures moving silently among the underbrush; see them navigate the thorns only to emerge on the other side ready to run and dance with joy. Look to the mountains above and on either side. Can you feel their majesty? Note the moving beams of bright sunshine on their peaks, *above the rocks.*

Do not be anxious to climb those mountains just yet. You will find your path to the summit a little later, but for now linger a little longer beside the stream, noting the provision made for the fish and the beauty of the sunlight as it dances across the waters. Rest in the beauty of God's creation.

Seek to understand the purpose of the rocks in the stream…could they actually be a form of protection and direction needed? Oh, if we would only remind ourselves that difficulties are not allowed without purpose and choose not to be overcome with dismay or feelings of defeat.

If we cannot understand the purpose can we truly burst forth onto God's path for a life with enthusiasm, with purpose, with God's vision? Can we sing the beautiful songs? Never forget that if God is allowed to choose the path, there will always be hope for each and every new day. You must be the one to continue walking forward to find the hope.

I am reminded of the ending lines of Alfred Lord Tennyson's "Charge of the Light Brigade."

> *'Forward, the Light Brigade!'*
> *Was there a man dismay'd?*
> *Not tho' the soldier knew*
> *Someone had blunder'd:*
> *Theirs not to make reply,*
> *Theirs not to reason why,*
> *Theirs but to do and die..."*

And I might add...die to Self
Recognize God has a plan and follow in faith.

The connection may take a minute; understanding takes time: Move forward in your faith, your determination, your prayers. Forward, never giving up. Let the Light be Jesus. Use your times of sadness or discipline to become a light for others, proving to yourself and others that God is, and always will be faithful. Choose to continue your walk through this valley. You have found yourself here for a reason, and that may include the recognition of God in your life at *all* times. It may be to teach you that God is always God, and God can create beauty in everything. It may be to identify the "rocks" that were needed to redirect your path. Your stroll along the stream may be the guide you need at just this moment; it may remind you that there are always opportunities to learn, to regain your strength, to feed on the truth God provides. The beautiful sunshine may just warm your heart as you are reminded of the joys along your way, in the midst of life's difficulties.

Be grateful for times of rest and sudden understanding.

Say thank you for times of instruction. Treasure the opportunities given. Accept the discipline. Know that God is always present. Use all to the glory of God. And choose to see Him in the midst of all your circumstances…

As you put aside the distress, the arguments of unfairness, the continual questions despite already knowing the answers…As you choose to follow in hopes of understanding God's purpose…As you put aside your arguments of "this is unfair" or your pleading questions of "why?" As you choose to place your faith in God, focus on Him and His mercy, be willing to "die" to your pride, your rebellion and accept that obedience to God in the midst of difficulty is always the best course of action.

Know that Action Requires Effort. Never give up or quit. Express your gratitude for the beautiful sunlight dancing on the waters. And continue on. Continue on to the see the grace and mercy of God that lies ahead.

And I close with one short extension of Oswald Chambers' earlier words: *"Then as surely as God is God, and you are you, you will turn out to be the exact likeness of the vision."* God's vision.

> *"No temptation has seized you except*
> *what is common to man.*
> *And God is faithful. He will not let you be*
> *tempted beyond what you can bear.*
> *But when you are tempted, He will also provide a*
> *way out so that you can stand up under it."*
> I Corinthians 10:13 NIV

18

And the Words of God still carry Hope. And the Praises Must Still Ring

While Your Testimony Encourages Others.

"Blessed is the man who makes the Lord his trust, who does not turn to the proud, to those who go astray after a lie." Psalm 40:4 ESV

There is the lie that 'evil has overcome the world.'
It has not.

It is certainly growing; it has certainly tried,
but only God is still God.

Only He has the power to redeem this world –
physically, spiritually, and lovingly.

Perhaps it is up to us to acknowledge His power.

To teach of His power,
and to become His Christian Soldiers in daily life.

At that point, I do believe the word is "Onward!"

**"You have multiplied, O Lord, my
God, Your wondrous deeds and
Your thoughts toward us. None can compare with You!
I will proclaim and tell of them. Yet, they are
more than can be told." Psalm 40:5 ESV**

19

Speechless or Grateful?

"Let my tongue stick to the roof of my mouth,
if I do not remember You..."
Psalm 136:6 NIV

Is it easier to remember the difficulties or the joyous, life-changing moments when God entered our difficult situations or struggles, when He acted as only God could, and you were able to relax? Your answers may vary, but my next question will go something like this – "what was the topic of your next conversation – the struggle or the blessing?"

Sharing the difficulties, even in times of "prayer requests" tends to have one share stories of hardship first. And that initial introduction to the topic just seems to *require* full detail, all emotional reactions, all righteous indignation, and all desires for sympathy. Am I right? Only then is God recognized for the recovery, the comfort, the miracle that seemed to 'put things right." And how long does that praise of God last? Honestly...?

If intent of the prayer request is to give full honor to the problem many feel the need to repeat the struggle as a means of giving God the glory of resolving the issue. But! Is the struggle the important part? Or is God's intervention, instruction, blessing the part we should be emphasizing? Evaluate your (probably unrecognized) organization. Be honest here.

What if you and I began our Prayer Requests, whether to friends or a group or even to God with an acknowledgement of *what God is doing* in this moment, to address our struggle, or to use that struggle to teach us valuable lessons? What if *"God is"* or *"God did"* became the headline rather than the struggle taking priority? For one thing, the prayer request would be shorter – after all, addressing all that God has, is or will be doing is really all that needs to be said, right? However, would we feel cheated out of the unspoken requests for sympathy for the speaker or would some be cheated out of the story-telling factor in the horror of the circumstances? Would someone in the group respond with, "Wait a minute! We already gave our Praises…why didn't you say this sooner?" It is a time to laugh, people. And in many cases to laugh at oneself. But to also address our priorities…

Acknowledge what God is doing in this moment to address the struggle, or to use that struggle to teach us valuable lessons.

One personal note: I tend to be emotional, thrilled to accept the presence of God in my daily life. And I just want to express that excitement. Would others consider me to have that poise to calmly express myself? No, certainly not. God is the source of my excitement, and I believe it can be contagious, so I simply do not want to give it up. On the other hand, my mother was an incredible woman, strong in her faith and poised in her response to frustration, hurt, concern, etc. She never quite understood my displays of emotion.

I sometimes look back and wish I had exhibited her poise during my teenage years.

I needed to express my fears and confusion and uncertainties of life on a regular basis. However, I recognized years ago that if I considered the worst-case scenario and could live with the consequences then I would be strong enough to move forward, regardless of circumstances. And then my Bible reassured me that God is always in control, and that with a little faith there really is no worst-case scenario. He has no plans to destroy us. As my faith grew, I began to realize that the real issue is not my choice to continue on but exactly how grateful would I feel when God stepped in to prevent total failure or catastrophe? If that is the true focus, the chosen focus then I do not need to spend quite as much time on the struggles but can move more quickly to the celebration of God in my life!

The real issue becomes, exactly how grateful would I feel when God stepped in to prevent total failure or catastrophe.

Couldn't everyone benefit from that? No more *unending* misery. No more *unending* fear. Instead, all can benefit from *unending* hope based in the One who can never fail. With

God by our side…Wow, how would you end that sentence? Think about it and smile!

Please do not misinterpret any of the previous thoughts. I am not suggesting we feel shame if our minds are not filled with lollipops and rainbows at all times. It is important that everyone have a confidant, a friend or counselor to discuss struggles with. Period. My intent is never to belittle that need. I believe that one must expel negative emotions before the positive ones can take root in the soul. I believe in total honesty with God, even when it means I respectfully ask why. I know that hope is never lost when God is allowed to work, and I admit to having to ask for His encouragement in remembering that statement.

What I am suggesting is that when God grants the blessing, extends the wisdom, comforts the soul it is only fitting that He receives the gratitude. He deserves the "Thank You, Lord!" rather than the never-ending "Woe is me…". He understands it may take time to reach that overwhelming, exhilarating Thank You, but we must also accept that we will never reach that joy if we do not begin – no matter how small that beginning may be. Sometimes the recognition of God's ability to protect us is enough. Other times, we would benefit from rehearsing those words: "Thank You, Lord" so that when the problems have become a thing of the past, we will know instantly how to shout "Thank You, Lord!" with all the exuberance we truly feel.

Psalm 137:4 ESV begins with the sub-heading "How Shall We Sing the Lord's Song?" Verses 1-3 lists the hardships God's people have suffered – Babylonian captivity, and the destruction of Jerusalem, times of sadness and recognition that God's people forgot their blessings. Yet, God never failed. Verse 6 continues with "Let my tongue stick to the roof of my mouth, if I do not remember you..." Let us never forget the grace and mercy and love of God even in the midst of hardship. Most importantly, let us never forget to praise the One who made all things possible. Therefore, how shall we sing God's praises?

a. First of all, be aware that "every good gift and every perfect gift is from above, coming down from the Father of lights with whom there is no variation or shadow due to change," James 1:7 ESV.

b. Second, every request for favor carries with it an obligation to express gratitude.

c. Third, choose to see the blessings regardless of the surrounding struggles.

d. Fourth, tell others of God and His mercies first and foremost. If you need to describe the circumstances of a struggle do so quickly and then acknowledge God's ensuing intervention. **Allow your praises and gratitude to take center stage, to take the spotlight, and allow God to take the bows without feeling any competition from you.**

Personal moment here: As I write the list above, I am just a few feet away from my Bible resting on the kitchen counter. It is an incredibly pleasant day, one that deserves my attention, so all windows are open. For the last thirty minutes I have heard a sound I could not identify. I listened to the roof vent, considered it could be the dog even though he had already taken up residence on his blanket in the closet, went to the back door to see if leaves were being blown about in the breeze, checked to see if papers on the dining room table were being rearranged. None would have been irritating, but the detective in me simply wanted to identify the sound. What I found was my Bible laying on the breakfast bar with pages being turned in the breeze!

What a visual! The pages of my Bible were open and capturing my attention; I had the choice to stop and read, simply close the nearest window, or complain about the interruption.

The choice was mine; the insight could be used for God or not. Therefore, one final item on my list.

e. Continually refer to your Bible so that you can become aware of all the ways, all the times, all the guidance that will allow you to see God's hands throughout your days. Perhaps there is much, much more for you to be grateful for! Perhaps the sheer magnitude of His blessings will begin to fill your mind and heart, and the difficulties will become smaller and occupy less of your time while your excitement simply must be expressed!

Let the above suggestions guide your days this week. Make a conscious effort to understand today's events, to survive this difficult time in the history of our world, and to recognize that God is still on His throne; Jesus is still remembering all He died to save, and the Holy Spirit may just be working overtime to help us understand that all is not lost. Use this day to refocus your attention and see that God's blessings still remain. We may just have to choose to look a little harder. And most importantly, God will always allow you to see, to know, and to accept that He is only waiting for your Invitation to be a gracious part of life as you know it.

Don't forget to rehearse the "Thank You, Lord" then Stand and Celebrate the goodness of God!

20

———✦———

Playin' the Games Of Life

"What if...?

One additional note: I looked for Bible verses containing "What if" and found only four in the NIV. Of the verses found, only one truly made me pause and realize the absolute, precious magnitude of the idea contained within.

> *"For what if some did not believe?*
> *Shall their unbelief make the faith*
> *of God without effect?"*
> Romans 3:3 NIV

Perhaps the bargaining phrase "what if" is the creation of human insecurity...a condition healed only by taking a chance on God and finding your trust has been well-placed.

21

~~~~

Makin' the Climb

"I waited patiently for the Lord; He
inclined to me and heard my cry.
He drew me up from the pit of destruction...
and set my feet on a rock, making my steps secure."
Psalm 40:1-2 ESV

Okay, Big Mountain, Here I Come!
Yes, Lord, I tried to prepare, packed the
essentials: spiritual food from my Bible,
water of life, humility and maybe
just a bit of chocolate.
Now, Lord, could you direct my path, please?

Understand that you get to choose to keep on climbing or stagger down in defeat. The Guide is holding your elbow with grace and mercy, and certainly providing constant reminders that He is nearby to help. You need never feel that you are alone through the struggles.

**Never forget! The reward is at the top.
The regret, the sense of failure, the
dissatisfaction is at the bottom.**

There is one important point that I absolutely *must* direct all your thoughts to! This chapter title implies that the journey to the top of the mountain will be a struggle, a wearying, strenuous, tear-filled, muscle-stretching, arduous effort on your part. Perhaps in other circumstances, I would agree. But this time the climb is different. And thus, this chapter is different, shorter than those that have come before.

This climb will be simple, joyous, and accompanied by Jesus. That is, if you will only allow it. This climb recognizes the Source of all Joy. The Source of Eternal Life. The Source of Strength and Encouragement and Hope. The only equipment needed is your profession of faith in the one, true God, and an acceptance of the love and forgiveness offered by Jesus – to you – on the Cross. It requires a simple yes or no answer…all else can follow throughout time. That one simple "yes" will equip you with joy, anticipation, and the motivation to continue your climb – to reach the life you truly desire.

Yes, there may be rocks, but you will begin to see them differently. There may be fatigue, but the faith in knowing Jesus will provide all the energy needed to keep you moving. Maybe even dancing! There will be joy unlike any you have ever imagined!

Never forget that true safety also includes letting others know where you are going! Share your journey. Inspire others with your hope. Teach others with your strength. Let others encourage you in times of fear, but never deny Who is waiting for you at the top. Share the wonders awaiting you when you reach your final destination at the top!

22

Shoutin' from the Mountain Tops!

"How beautiful on the mountain are the feet of those who bring good news, who proclaim peace, who bring good tidings, who proclaim salvation."
Isaiah 52:7 ESV

Dance and shout; hold your hands in the air and twirl as you praise God and shout about the joy that others are looking for – you know that joy – God gave it – now know that others need it as well – So Share!

Perhaps it was a hard climb to get there.
Perhaps it is the unknown.
Perhaps someone told you after that
there is nowhere to go but down –
you tell them the only one true God is higher still.

**God is in Heaven, and all is so, so, so, good.
No fear, just pure unadulterated joy!**

Avoid the temptation to play "King of the Mountain" and take the credit for your successful climb. Do not attempt to be the focus point of the mountaintop - God is. By the way, God should have also been the focus in the Valley – even if you are just now realizing that. It is time to let your words of praise and testimony ring out!

Let others understand that hope is never lost. Please know, the one thing that you and I must avoid, and protect others from, is the feeling of despair, of loss of hope, of anger, of defeat. Did God leave us? No. Does He ever? No. He is still here, and He asks that you reassure others of that fact. This is your chance to share your faith with others – it is needed now more than ever.

It is time to let others know God is the One who invited you to this beautiful summit. And, just as important, let them know you have invited God to be a part of your world! It is time to encourage others to do the same!

Your voice is needed. Life is unpredictable and often overwhelming. Most of us fail many times throughout our lives. Have you? **If** you are willing to recognize the true source of your struggles and acknowledge the God of Glory who truly enables you to emerge victorious **then** you have a truly incredible testimony! Truly… Others do not want to see your supposed perfection; they need to see their struggles are not unique. They need to know the One who led you to the understanding and saving grace that made your survival possible.

In the year 2020 the world experienced a pandemic

on a scale no one could have ever imagined. Illness, death, uncertainty in the areas of medical care, employment... changes in government, changes in education, changes in home environments.

We are still seeing death, destruction, loss of hope, and subsequent health issues. It is heart-breaking. The U.S. has lost so many wonderful and *valuable* people, and *now we continue to see the even greater tragedy in the ongoing loss of many individuals who have not had the opportunity to know Jesus and to become all that God intended for them to be.* Is this the world any of us would have chosen? No. Is this the world we are living in? Yes. So, what are we to do about it?

**Stop and pray! Turn and Listen. Live
and Learn, and then Teach.**

**Praise God in your words, in your actions,
and most of all in your hearts.
Feel and Share His Compassion.
Express Gratitude for God's Love and Mercy.
Tell of the wonders of His Son, Jesus.
And ask Him – sincerely – to use you
as His witness in this world.
And then become the person He can use.**

**Teach the good news that is spread
throughout your Bible.
Share the importance of faith –
and share the joy of knowing God
will always be with us!**

Do not question your ability to share, to teach, to love...

that is a waste of time. You are already equipped to do as God has or will ask. That is FACT. You have already been given the all-important message that others are needing to here.

You have been blessed. Now, it is time to share!

Works Cited

Chambers, Oswald. Editor: James Reimann. <u>My Utmost for His Highest Updated Edition</u>. Oswald Chambers Publications Association Ltd, 1992. (July 6 entry).

Elliott, C and Bradbury, W.B. "Just As I Am." <u>The Baptist Hymnal</u>. Nashville, Tenness, Convention Press.303.

Hummel, Charles E. <u>Tyranny of the Urgent</u>. Downers Grove, Illinois: Inter-Varsity Press, Rev. ed. 1994.

Maxwell, John C. <u>Attitude 101: What Every Leader Needs to Know</u>. Nashville: Thomas Nelson Publishers. 2003. (4).

Thomas, Gary L. <u>Sacred Pathways, Discover your Soul's Path to God</u>. Zondervan. 1996. (18).